Shortcuts to Success

Hamlet

EXAM GUIDE FOR LEAVING CERTIFICATE

Anne Gormley

Gill & Macmillan

Gill & Macmillan
Hume Avenue
Park West
Dublin 12
with associated companies throughout the world
www.gillmacmillan.ie
© Anne Gormley, 2010
978 07171 4727 4

Print origination in Ireland by O'K Graphic Design, Dublin

The paper used in this book is made from the wood pulp of managed forests. For every tree felled, at least one tree is planted, thereby renewing natural resources.

ACKNOWLEDGMENTS

I wish to thank the late Eilish O Brien for allowing me to use her notes on *Hamlet*, and for all her help and support.

Contents

Background Notes on *Hamlet*   1

The Notion of Shakespearean Tragedy   2

The Soliloquy in Shakespeare's Tragedies   4

Hamlet as a Tragic Play   5

The Plot of *Hamlet*   6

Summary/Analysis of Scenes   7

Character Analysis   21

    Hamlet   21

    Claudius   25

    Gertrude   29

    Ophelia   33

    The Ghost   36

    Polonius   41

    Horatio   43

    Laertes   45

    Fortinbras   48

    Rosencrantz and Guildenstern   49

Themes   51

    False Appearance and Reality   51

    Power and Kingship   53

    Vengeance and Filial Duty   55

    The Mother Figure   60

    Death   64

Language and Imagery   68

Key Quotations and How to Use Them   75

Summary of Soliloquies and Asides   80

Some Key Situations   84

How to Study this Play   87

How to Answer Exam-style Questions   89

Sample Questions and Answers   92

Questions on *Hamlet*   116

Department of Education Guidelines on Answering Leaving Cert Questions   118

BACKGROUND NOTES ON
HAMLET

Shakespeare was at the midpoint of his career around 1599. At this stage in his life he began to write in a more mature style. He had by this stage accumulated a great deal of experience, had encountered many new influences and had suffered losses in his life, all of which helped to generate a more heightened creativity.

The years from 1598 to 1601 were characterised by a new style and a leaning towards writing tragic plays. The changes in his style came about as a result of many different factors, including changes in contemporary politics and the existence of rivalries within the theatre—there were many new, budding writers at this time. As a playwright and artist, Shakespeare was always ahead of the rest.

In these years Shakespeare was reading some of the Greek dramas, including Aeschylus's tragedy *Oresteia*. It seems that this work may have inspired certain parts of *Hamlet*, such as the Graveyard and the Closet scenes, as well as the character of Horatio.

Hamlet seems to have been drafted in the year 1599. Like many of Shakespeare's plays, the plot was taken from an old play—this one probably written by Thomas Kyd in 1589, which included a ghost. Shakespeare changed his setting from the mediaeval pagan world to fifteenth-century Christian Denmark.

Hamlet was deliberately written as a revenge tragedy—this genre was popular at the time in Elizabethan England. The setting would have been very familiar to an Elizabethan audience—Wittenberg was known for its Protestant-leaning university, which was also Luther's alma mater.

The play *Hamlet* was first staged in 1600. It is interesting that Shakespeare's own father John Shakespeare died in September of 1601; and it is also interesting that his father had requested that the correct Catholic rites, such as saying Masses for the souls in purgatory, should be undertaken on his death. The ghost's insights into purgatory are certainly chilling, and they enable us to imagine Shakespeare's mindset in this period of his life.

Hamlet, one of the most critiqued or commented upon works of literature, is a splendid play in its delineation of personality and its portrayal of inwardness.

One of the earliest performances of *Hamlet* took place in September 1607 on board a ship called the *Dragon*, which was sailing along the coast of Sierra Leone in West Africa. There were many dignitaries among the audience.

THE NOTION OF SHAKESPEAREAN TRAGEDY

The two traditional forms of drama are comedy and tragedy. Comedy laughs at humanity's disruptive instincts and passions: tragedy, on the other hand, analyses the motivations behind people's actions, in particular those that disrupt the social order. The results of this disruption lead to the death of the main protagonist—in tragedy, the conclusion is always the death of the leading character. There is also a strong focus on the causes of evil in humankind. This evil is rooted in personal freedom and results in death—not only of the bad characters, but also of the innocent.

All great tragedies force us to ask some very important questions. First of all, can virtue and good qualities survive in a world that seems to be dominated by evil and destruction?

What place does freedom have in the whole question of evil-doing? How much does the will of the person influence their behaviour, particularly when they do wrong?

Hamlet is one of Shakespeare's four main tragedies (the others are *Othello*, *King Lear* and *Macbeth*). In the play, we witness how Hamlet is confronted from early on with a huge moral dilemma—he is ordered to avenge the murder of his father. Claudius, the King of Denmark and Hamlet's uncle, is a corrupt monarch who has attained the throne by murdering his own brother. Hamlet is unable to appeal to law or justice as Claudius is the law and represents justice through his role as monarch.

The story of Polonius and his two children, Laertes and Ophelia, form the subject matter of the subplot. Both plots merge at different stages throughout this play, and, as in all Shakespeare's tragedies, the culmination of the action in this play results in the deaths of all the leading protagonists.

There is a basic **pattern** in tragedy.

- The tragic hero is generally a person who plays a prominent role in the social order, such as a king, a general, a great soldier.
- This person has a huge capacity for achieving heroic acts and moral greatness.
- Through his use of freedom and conscience his life is thrown into confusion and discord.
- This sense of confusion and discord extends to all his relationships, and all aspects of his life.
- This sense of discord or disharmony is generally of an **extreme** nature.

- Life becomes chaotic and meaningless for the main protagonist.
- The tragic hero reaches a state of recognition about the implications of his flaw for himself and his life in general.
- The action culminates in the death of the tragic hero.
- Good triumphs at the conclusion and the forces of evil are vanquished, but not without causing a great deal of harm to the body politic.

So there is a certain movement in tragedy. The tragic hero moves from a state of high status —professionally, socially, morally, psychologically, etc.—downward through **suffering**. Part of the tragic process involves the tragic hero's **perception** of the implications of his flaw on both his own life and on those of the people around him. This perception or **insight** on the part of the tragic hero is important as it enables the audience to retain sympathy with him even in a state of destitution and loss.

Tragedy also deals with **realistic events and realistic people**. The audience must be able to identify with and understand the emotions reflected in a tragedy. Usually the tragic hero's flaw involves a misjudgment or an error of some type, and this is made by a person **with full freedom**, conscious about what they are doing and conscious about the consequences.

It is essential that the dramatist can gain the sympathy of the audience for the tragic hero. This presupposes that an audience can identify with the hero and recognise in him a similar humanity and capacity for both greatness and error. The tragic hero must be a person who can stand for us and reflect all aspects of our human nature.

THE SOLILOQUY IN SHAKESPEARE'S TRAGEDIES

The soliloquy in all drama is a speech by a character which is addressed to the audience. Drama is an ideal form for the soliloquy as an actor can face an audience directly from the stage and convey emotion through facial expressions and bodily gestures.

The soliloquy in Shakespeare would have been addressed to an Elizabethan audience on a stage which protruded into the pit: the audience would have been sitting (or standing in some cases) on three sides. This afforded Shakespeare an excellent means of developing the plot of his dramas. By means of the soliloquy, an audience can enter into the mind of a character and begin to understand the various emotions and conflicts within that person. The soliloquy gives an audience an insight into a character's soul and the inner workings of his or her mindset, which are more difficult to perceive in dialogue. Through the language and imagery used in a soliloquy, an audience can see, hear and feel all that a character is expressing. The soliloquy becomes a very powerful means of showing character and motivation, and of developing the plot.

THE ASIDE

Like the soliloquy, an aside is a short speech that is expressed by a character directly to the audience. It differs in length from the soliloquy, but in general it has the same function, which is to give the audience an insight into the soul and motivations of a character.

See page 80 for a summary of the soliloquies and the asides that appear in the play.

HAMLET AS A TRAGIC PLAY

In his book *Poetics*, Aristotle maintained that tragic drama is an imitation of life. For Aristotle, tragedy is 'an imitation of an action which is serious and complete, and which has a kind of magnitude . . . it is dramatic and not narrative in form. Through pity and fear it accomplishes a purgation of the emotions.'

Shakespeare manages to do this in his play *Hamlet*. The play shows us the tragic consequences of a corrupt monarchy. We are offered though tragic catharsis a view of human motivation in some very complex situations, and also the experience of death. The play shows us the power of love, and loyalty, and encourages us through our survival to bear all things well and to keep going.

The story begins with the death of Old Hamlet and the election of his brother Claudius to the throne of Denmark. Young Hamlet knows that something is wrong. This is confirmed when he meets the Ghost, who turns out to be his father. The Ghost orders him to avenge his foul, unnatural murder. The play is based on Hamlet's attempts to put this command into practice. We witness the consequences of young Hamlet's efforts to avenge the murder of his own beloved father.

THE PLOT OF *HAMLET*

The plot of the play is centred on the death of Old Hamlet, former King of Denmark. Old Hamlet's brother immediately succeeds to the throne and proceeds to marry Gertrude, Old Hamlet's widow and the mother of young Hamlet. The atmosphere is rife with suspicion and corruption. The court is filled with lies, infidelity and corruption. There are hints of war and revolution from outside Denmark, while the Ghost's appearance brings omens of revenge and destruction coming from the other world of purgatory.

From the moment when young Hamlet meets with his father Old Hamlet, who tells him to revenge his foul, unnatural murder by his brother Claudius, the play moves speedily to its tragic and dramatic conclusion.

Shakespeare makes clever use of the soliloquy to reveal the inner mindset and thoughts of his characters.

SUMMARY/ANALYSIS OF SCENES

ACT I, SCENE I

This scene takes place at night outside the castle of Elsinore in Denmark. Two guards, Francisco and Barnardo, are on the platform on duty. They speak about the appearance of a ghost, who was dressed in military attire and resembled Old Hamlet, the king, who has just died. When Horatio arrives they both tell him about the ghost. Horatio informs them about the political situation; how the former King of Norway was slain in combat by Old Hamlet and was forced to relinquish his lands as part of the settlement. Young Fortinbras, the King of Norway's son, has now gathered together an army in order to regain those lands lost by his father, and for that reason the Danish people are awaiting an attack. As they speak, the Ghost make its appearance but says nothing. The cock crows and the Ghost immediately disappears. The scene concludes with Horatio's announcement that he will inform young Hamlet about the appearance of the Ghost.

Questions

1. In Shakespeare's plays, Act I Scene i introduces us to the key elements in the drama as a whole. This is particularly true of the first scene in *Hamlet*. Discuss this statement.
2. What is Horatio's function in this scene?
3. What have we learned about the state of Denmark by the end of this first scene?

ACT I, SCENE II

This scene takes place inside the castle of Elsinore. We meet Claudius, who has been newly appointed as King of Denmark, with his wife Gertrude. Young Hamlet is there amidst the courtiers and dignitaries. He is dressed in black as he is mourning the death of his father, Old Hamlet. Claudius has just assumed the throne of Denmark because of his brother's recent death. Claudius is giving a political speech before the Danish court to justify his hasty marriage to Gertrude in the light of his brother's recent death just two months ago. Claudius speaks about the political threat posed by young Fortinbras and how he has managed to avert war by appealing to the uncle of Fortinbras to stop the threatened violence against Denmark. Claudius consolidates this achievement by sending out two ambassadors, Cornelius and Voltemand, to ensure peace between both countries.

We begin to realise in this scene what a shrewd political operator Claudius is. He manages to deal with everyone tactfully and skilfully. Laertes, the son of Polonius, who is the main Counsellor of State, requests leave to return to France, and Claudius gives him permission to do so. Meanwhile, Claudius addresses young Hamlet, who answers him negatively and ambiguously. Claudius begins to urge Hamlet to abandon his grief for his father and resume his life—he is being obstinate in not accepting the will of heaven. Gertrude joins Claudius in pleading with Hamlet to stay in Denmark and to cease mourning. Hamlet agrees.

When everyone has left the court, Hamlet engages in a soliloquy in which he tells us how wretched life is; it is like an 'unweeded garden' in which there are 'things rank and gross in nature'. Hamlet is clearly deeply upset about his father's death and his mother's frailty in remarrying so quickly.

Horatio arrives and informs Hamlet about the appearance of the Ghost on the platform. Hamlet decides to watch that night, stating that he believes some foul play is afoot.

Questions

1. What impression is Claudius trying to make on the court, and where are you most aware of this speech as being aimed for 'public consumption'?
2. Discuss the importance of Hamlet's appearance, before we hear him speak in this scene. What is Shakespeare concerned to establish from the outset here?
3. What do Gertrude's words reveal about her attitudes to death, to widowhood and to her first husband?
4. Sum up what is revealed about Hamlet's state of mind in his first soliloquy. What do you see as key phrases or lines in this soliloquy? Comment on Hamlet's initial reaction to Horatio's arrival.

ACT I, SCENE III

In this scene Laertes is bidding farewell to his sister Ophelia before he embarks for France. (The activities of Polonius and his two children Laertes and Ophelia form part of the subplot of the play.) Before Laertes leaves he makes a series of moral statements to his sister about her relationship with Hamlet. He tells her not to lose her virtue, since Hamlet is subject to his royal birth and is not permitted to choose for himself when it comes to marriage. Ophelia agrees to follow her brother's advice on condition that he will not act like a hypocritical pastor who is showing her how to get to heaven but is acting like a reckless libertine himself.

When Polonius enters he blesses his son before his journey and gives him a series of counsels to help him when he is abroad. These pieces of advice are generally designed to foster self-interest and self-love. He tells his son to 'Take every man's censure, but reserve thy judgment,' and above all, 'to thine own self be true . . . thou canst not then be false to any man'.

Laertes leaves for France and Polonius cautions Ophelia about her relationship with Hamlet, telling her that she is inexperienced and innocent, a 'green girl', to avoid giving her time to Hamlet and to ignore him instead. Ophelia reluctantly agrees.

Questions

1. How would you describe Polonius's attitude to fatherhood as demonstrated here?
2. Is Laertes really concerned with morality in advising Ophelia as he does? Examine the language he uses as an indication of his underlying approach.
3. What is the importance of the line 'To thine own self be true . . . thou canst not then be false to any man'?

ACT I, SCENE IV

This scene takes place at night on the platform before the castle. Hamlet has arrived with Horatio and Marcellus with the intention of meeting the Ghost and finding out what is happening. They hear trumpets and the sound of the cannon firing. Horatio explains that celebrations are taking place and that this has been a custom for many years now. The Ghost appears and beckons Hamlet to follow it. Horatio warns Hamlet that it may be evil and tells him not to go. Hamlet declares that his life is worthless—'I do not set my life at a pin's fee'—and decides to follow the Ghost. This scene concludes with Hamlet following the Ghost while Marcellus declares that 'Something is rotten in the state of Denmark.'

Questions

1. What is the importance of Hamlet's lengthy speech condemning the drinking habits prevalent among the Danes?
2. Discuss Hamlet's initial reaction to the Ghost's appearance.
3. What unexpected aspect of Hamlet's nature is revealed at this point in the scene? At what other points in the play does he behave in a similar fashion? What do you think Shakespeare wants to suggest to us here?

ACT I, SCENE V

In this scene Hamlet speaks to the Ghost, who tells him to revenge the 'foul' and 'unnatural' murder of Claudius. The Ghost then reveals that he is Hamlet's father, and that he was murdered while he slept in his garden. He tells Hamlet that he has come from purgatory, where he is suffering for his sins. The Ghost explains that Hamlet must carry out the revenge without endangering his mother: she is merely to be punished by heaven, by 'those thorns that in her bosom lodge/To prick and sting her'.

Hamlet is traumatised and immediately decides that the only idea that will remain in his brain is the Ghost's command to revenge. When Horatio and Marcellus return they are anxious to find out what information was conveyed by the ghost. Hamlet is hysterical and erratic in his behaviour and they chastise him for his 'wild and whirling words'. Hamlet gets them to swear not to disclose anything to anyone about the events of that night. He also tells them that he will adopt 'an antic disposition'. The scene concludes with Hamlet cursing the fact that he is the one called on to remedy the disjointed state of things in Denmark.

Questions

1. Consider the Ghost's attitude to (a) revenge; (b) Claudius; (c) Gertrude.
2. The Ghost's revelations throw Hamlet off balance: how is his instability conveyed?
3. 'The time is out of joint … set it right.' What do these words at the close of the scene indicate about Hamlet's view of what has now been revealed to him?

ACT II, SCENE I

This scene takes place in the house of Polonius. Polonius is speaking to his servant Reynaldo and telling him to take some money to his son Laertes in France. He then goes on to ask Reynaldo to find out in a devious way what Laertes is doing in France—what company he is keeping and the lifestyle he is sustaining. Polonius wants Reynaldo to use lies in order to fish out the truth about his son. When Reynaldo leaves, Ophelia enters. She announces that she has just met Hamlet, who appeared to her in a state of distress, with his clothes dishevelled, and who seems to be in a state of madness. Ophelia is horrified and deeply distressed. Polonius tells her that Hamlet's behaviour is due to his love for her and the fact that she has rejected him. Polonius decides to inform Claudius about this incident.

Questions

1. What is Polonius's view of Laertes here?
2. What is the thematic significance of the statement, 'by indirections find directions out'?
3. What was Hamlet's purpose in confronting Ophelia in this fashion?

ACT II, SCENE II

This scene, the longest scene in the play, takes place in the castle of Elsinore. It opens with Claudius welcoming Rosencrantz and Guildenstern to Elsinore. These two are old school friends of Hamlet, and Claudius would like them to stay in the palace in order to befriend Hamlet and discover what is wrong with him, as he is 'too much changed'.

The ambassadors Voltemand and Cornelius return from Denmark with good news that Young Fortinbras has been ordered by his uncle to stop his war against Denmark and to fight the Polish instead. Claudius is asked to give access to Fortinbras's army through Denmark to help him attack the Poles. Claudius is delighted with this news.

Polonius arrives and informs Claudius about Hamlet's recent behaviour, telling him that it is due to unrequited love. Claudius is doubtful about this theory but agrees to use Ophelia as bait in order to uncover the real truth about Hamlet's state of mind. They both decide to hide behind an 'arras' or tapestry while Hamlet meets with Ophelia.

Hamlet appears and begins to mock Polonius, telling him he is a 'fishmonger'. When Hamlet meets Rosencrantz and Guildenstern he is unsure about their intentions in the palace. He tries to get them to tell him the real reasons why they are in Elsinore. Guildenstern finally tells him that they were 'sent for'. Then Hamlet informs them that he has felt depressed lately and is tired with life. While the two of them look on, Hamlet mocks Polonius, calling him 'Jephthah', a reference to a corrupt judge from the Bible.

The players arrive and they act out a small drama before Hamlet about Pyrrhus avenging the death of his father Achilles. The players dramatise this incident from Trojan history with profound emotion—one of the players actually cries while acting. This incident leads to a strong soliloquy from Hamlet which concludes this scene. In this soliloquy Hamlet engages in a deep sense of self-reproach, condemning himself for his tardiness, or slowness, in avenging his father's death. He does, however, express his doubt about the Ghost being a devil. Hamlet decides to stage a play that night which will re-enact the details of Old Hamlet's murder and thereby he hopes to 'catch the conscience of the king'.

Questions

1. Comment on the importance of the Pyrrhus speech.
2. Hamlet appears to get the idea of the play on the spur of the moment: is this typical of his behaviour?
3. What is revealed of Hamlet's state of mind in the soliloquy that concludes this scene?

ACT III, SCENE I

In this scene, which could be called the Nunnery Scene, Claudius and Polonius both use Ophelia as bait in order to trap Hamlet and uncover what lies underneath his unusual behaviour. Polonius gives Ophelia a pious book to use as a cover or excuse so that Hamlet will not suspect that Claudius and Polonius are listening to the conversation.

Hamlet enters and begins to speak about life and death in the famous speech 'To be, or not to be.' Immediately after this he meets Ophelia and begins to speak quite violently to her, questioning her honesty and her 'paintings' or efforts at deceit. It seems clear that he suspects already that she is being used as a dupe by her father and Claudius. He is quite aggressive and angry, and tells her to go to a nunnery and leave him alone. Ophelia interprets his behaviour as that of a mad person and laments the destruction of his fine intellectual faculties. When Hamlet has left, Claudius and Polonius enter. It is clear that Claudius realises that Hamlet is not really mad but that there is something troubling him, and he (Claudius) will do his utmost to watch him from now on, telling Polonius how, 'Madness in great ones must not unwatched go.'

Questions

1. Why precisely is Claudius's aside so significant when Polonius speaks about deception?
2. Is Hamlet justified in behaving towards Ophelia as he does?
3. Why are Hamlet's references to 'painting' significant?
4. 'O! what a noble mind is here o'erthrown.' What does this speech tell us about Hamlet? About Ophelia herself?
5. When Claudius and Polonius enter, they ignore the weeping Ophelia. What point is being made here?

ACT III, SCENE II

In this scene Hamlet stages the play called 'The Mousetrap', and manages to expose Claudius's guilt. Hamlet is skilled in the theatre and loves it, so this effort to stage a play enacting the murder of his father is a complete success. Initially the players act a dumb show, simply moving around the stage and miming the process of the murder. Hamlet has engineered things so that Claudius, who is sitting at the front watching the performance with Gertrude, will be exposed clearly. When the actors begin to pour poison into the ear of the sleeping king, Claudius rises and asks for some light. He is greatly agitated and runs away, 'frighted with false fire' as Hamlet claims. Hamlet is ecstatic because he now has confirmation that the Ghost's words are true. When Rosencrantz and Guildenstern arrive to tell him that his mother has summoned him to her, Hamlet treats them with contempt. He begins to attack them both, chastising them for trying to use him like a pipe and trying to 'pluck out the heart of my mystery'.

The scene concludes with Hamlet announcing that he will 'speak daggers to her [his mother], but use none'. He plans to confront his mother with her guilt now that he has managed to trap Claudius.

Questions

1. This scene is often regarded as the turning point of the play: discuss why this should be so.
2. How is Hamlet's state of mind changed by the events of this scene?
3. What is the significance of Hamlet labelling the play 'The Mousetrap'?
4. (a) How will the Court react to the king's rising? (b) Claudius asks for *light*: discuss the symbolic element here.
5. What is the effect of the final soliloquy in the scene? Is Hamlet deceiving himself about his own firmness of purpose?

ACT III, SCENE III

This scene could be called the Prayer Scene. Claudius orders both Rosencrantz and Guildenstern to take Hamlet out of Denmark immediately and set sail for England. Hamlet poses too great a threat to Claudius, so he must be removed.

Claudius goes to pray in his own private chapel or oratory. Here he is alone and is overwhelmed with guilt about having committed murder. He is unable to ask for mercy as he does not want to relinquish the fruits of his crime—'My crown, mine own ambition, and my queen'. He would like to be pardoned but also retain the fruits of his deed, and so he is struggling within himself.

Hamlet arrives while Claudius is kneeling in prayer and thinks that this is an ideal opportunity to avenge himself on Claudius and kill him. But Hamlet begins to consider that murdering Claudius while he is repenting will only speed him on to heaven, and will not be a suitable act of vengeance on Hamlet's part. He decides to catch Claudius in an act where he can be damned and go to hell. This is quite an ironic situation because the audience are aware that Claudius has been unable to repent of his deed and ask forgiveness.

Questions

1. Rosencrantz's speech—'The single and peculiar life ... with a general groan'—is of course intended to flatter, but it also makes a point which is significant in relation to the drama as a whole. Discuss.
2. For the first time in this drama, we find Claudius alone, and his soliloquy follows. What is the dramatic purpose of this episode?
3. Consider Hamlet's reaction to the sight of the king at prayer. What do you see as lying behind his failure to take the opportunity for revenge offered him at this point?
4. Discuss the irony of Claudius's final words in this scene: 'My words fly up ... to heaven go'.

ACT III, SCENE IV

This scene, which could be called the Closet Scene, takes place in Gertrude's bedroom. Polonius has arranged to hide behind a screen in Gertrude's room in order to overhear their conversation. When Hamlet enters, he begins to chastise his mother, telling her that he will show her a mirror so that she can see deep inside herself. Gertrude is frightened and begins to move towards the arras or screen. As she does so, Hamlet lashes out and attacks Polonius with his sword, killing him. Then he orally attacks his mother, telling her that she has managed to make marriage vows false by marrying her husband's brother so quickly after his death. Hamlet succeeds in getting Gertrude to acknowledge her guilt and sin as she tells him how she sees 'black and grained spots' in her soul. The Ghost appears while Hamlet is chastising his mother and announces to Hamlet that he has come to 'whet thy almost blunted purpose', in other words to encourage Hamlet to avenge the Ghost's death. It is interesting that only Hamlet can actually see the Ghost here—he is invisible to Gertrude. The Ghost also admonishes Hamlet to refrain from over-reacting to Gertrude:

she is suffering enough. This scene concludes with Hamlet telling his mother that he must now answer for the murder of Polonius.

Questions
1. 'As kill a king!' What does this tell us about Gertrude's character?
2. Where are you most aware of Hamlet as 'speaking daggers' to his mother?
3. What effect does the entry of the Ghost have on the mood and atmosphere of this episode?
4. Why does Gertrude not see the Ghost?
5. Consider the importance of Hamlet's reference to himself as 'scourge and minister'.
6. Is Hamlet's behaviour to his mother in this episode (a) reasonable, (b) understandable?

ACT IV, SCENE I

In this scene, Claudius hears about the death of Polonius, his principal counsellor of state, at the hands of Hamlet. It is clear that Claudius is less concerned with the deed than with the consequences it will have on his own security and his life. All Claudius's words and actions speak of self-interest and self-preservation. He tells Gertrude that they must summon their wisest counsellors of state to see what is to be done.

Questions
1. In a staged performance of the play, there ought to be no distinct break between the final scene of Act III and the first scene of Act IV. Explain.
2. What are the king's main preoccupations in this scene? How characteristic is his attitude? What impression does he make on you here?
3. What does this brief scene contribute to the play?

ACT IV, SCENE II

Rosencrantz and Guildenstern have been asked to bring the body of Polonius to the king's chapel. They meet Hamlet and ask him about the body. Hamlet treats them with contempt, telling them he will not be demanded of by a 'sponge.'

Questions

1. Comment on the fact that Hamlet is still pretending madness in this scene.
2. In their exchange with Hamlet, the two courtiers continually address Hamlet as 'My lord'. What point is being made here?
3. What is the significance of Hamlet's reference to the king as 'a thing of nothing'? What effect will this comment have on those who hear it?

ACT IV, SCENE III

The king is intent on getting rid of Hamlet straight away, since he poses a direct threat to his own life. He tells Rosencrantz and Guildenstern that Hamlet must be sent away in a natural and organised manner. Hamlet meets with Claudius and refuses to engage in rational conversation, instead making a series of clever and ironic puns and ambiguous statements. The underlying purpose is to show that Hamlet despises and distrusts Claudius absolutely.

Claudius informs Hamlet that he must, for his own safety, set sail immediately for England with Rosencrantz and Guildenstern. Claudius secretly plans to have Hamlet killed in England.

Questions

1. 'He's loved of the distracted multitude . . . /But never the offence.' Why is this point important in relation to Hamlet?
2. 'To bear all smooth and even'. Why is this comment significant?
3. 'Diseases desperate grown ... or not at all.' Comment on Claudius's attitude here.
4. '... certain convocation of politic worms are e'en at him ...' What is Hamlet trying to achieve here in his emphasis on death and corruption?
5. (a) What does Claudius's final speech reveal? (b) 'Like the hectic in my blood he rages ...' Comment on the significance of the imagery here

ACT IV, SCENE IV

This scene takes place in Denmark as Hamlet prepares to leave for England. He sees an army led by Fortinbras crossing the land and preparing to fight for a small tract of land that in itself is worthless. Hamlet uses this opportunity to engage in another soliloquy, in which he compares himself to Fortinbras and recognises that while he, Hamlet, is still procrastinating over the deed, Fortinbras is prepared to sacrifice the lives of twenty thousand men for a mere piece of land that is not big enough to bury them all. Hamlet decides that from now on his deeds must be bloody.

Questions

1. Is it significant that we are presented with Fortinbras, however briefly, at this point in the drama? What impression does he make on us?
2. Where is disease imagery used in this scene and to what effect?
3. Hamlet's soliloquy is provoked by what he has just heard of Fortinbras. What has this soliloquy in common with the one following the player's speech? Why did Shakespeare introduce a soliloquy by Hamlet just at this point of the play's action?
4. Discuss the significance of Hamlet's final comment in this soliloquy.

ACT IV, SCENE V

This scene takes place in the castle of Elsinore. Ophelia, who by now is completely mad, wishes to meet with Gertrude. She enters and begins to sing several songs about lost love and betrayal. This incident leads to Claudius's speech in which he tells Gertrude how tragic things are: first the death of Polonius and now Ophelia, who is 'divided from herself and her fair judgment'. Claudius is overcome with emotion and does not know what to do.

Laertes has just heard of his sister's madness and his father's speedy death and burial, and returns to Denmark incensed at Claudius and deeply suspicious of him. It takes all of Claudius's fortitude to pacify him and make him an ally, not an enemy. The scene concludes with Claudius and Laertes colluding to avenge Polonius's death and Ophelia's madness.

Questions

1. What is revealed of the queen's state of mind here?
2. (a) Comment on Claudius's reaction to the spectacle of Ophelia's madness.
   (b) What important information do we gain during the course of Claudius's speech?
3. How does Claudius behave in this crisis? Comment on his reference to 'the divinity hedging a king'.
4. Ophelia bestows flowers on some of those present: what is Shakespeare's intention here?

ACT IV, SCENE VI

In this short scene, a servant hands Horatio letters from Hamlet, in which he tells Horatio that he has escaped from pirates at sea and that Rosencrantz and Guildenstern are heading for England. Hamlet asks Horatio to meet him and to give some letters to Claudius.

Questions

1. Has this scene any significance other than to keep us alert as to the plot development?
2. Consider the style of the letter: does it sound like the Hamlet we know?

ACT IV, SCENE VII

This scene takes place in the palace in Elsinore. During an exchange between Claudius and Laertes, the king uses every trick to manipulate Laertes over to his side and to convince him of Hamlet's guilt. As they are speaking, a messenger arrives with letters from Hamlet in which he addresses Claudius sarcastically and tells him he is returning to Denmark. Claudius is puzzled, but uses this as an opportunity to bully Laertes into murdering Hamlet in a duel which will be engineered against him.

Just as Claudius has managed to convince Laertes, the queen arrives with the news that Ophelia has drowned while climbing to collect some flowers. Her death would seem to be a suicide. The scene concludes with Laertes's strong determination to punish Hamlet.

Questions

1. What excuses does the king offer Laertes for not pursuing Hamlet more vigorously? How convincing is his first excuse?
2. 'But to the quick o' the ulcer'. What is the relevance of this phrase?
3. In devising the details of the plot, what are Claudius's chief concerns?
4. Comment on the queen's account of Ophelia's death.

ACT V, SCENE I

Act V is the concluding act, and it is made up of two scenes. The first scene takes place in a graveyard and could be termed the Graveyard Scene. At the opening, two gravediggers are preparing the ground for the burial of Ophelia and they are discussing whether or not she should receive a Christian burial, given that she took her own life. Some of their comments are deeply perceptive and filled with a lot of insight. They comment on how the houses built by a gravemaker last until doomsday.

Hamlet enters with Horatio and he also speaks about death, and corrupt politicians, and how death is a great leveller. Hamlet picks up a skull which is lying on the ground and which happens to be that of Yorick, the court jester when Hamlet was a young boy. He uses this situation to condemn false appearance and hypocrisy, saying aloud to the skull to go off to his lady's chamber and remind her that she too will end up as a skull in a graveyard in spite of all her efforts to hide behind her make-up. This turns out to be cruelly ironic because shortly afterwards Ophelia's dead body is brought into the graveyard, followed by her brother Laertes, her father Claudius, and Gertrude. Hamlet confronts Laertes, who is incensed because he blames Hamlet for the death of his sister. The king manages to separate the two fighting men and tells Gertrude to control her son while he pacifies Laertes by telling him that his opportunity for revenge will come very soon.

Questions

1. What does the conversation of the two gravediggers contribute to the play?
2. Hamlet has often thought about death in general. Now he finds Yorick's skull. How does this affect his attitude?
3. Consider the effect of Laertes's language and behaviour at this point.
4. (a) Discuss Hamlet's reaction to what Laertes says and does.
   (b) 'I loved Ophelia . . .' What lends tragic intensity to Hamlet's words here?
5. Comment on Claudius's words at the end of the scene.

ACT V, SCENE II

The concluding scene takes place inside the castle of Elsinore. At the beginning of the scene, Hamlet is telling Horatio how he managed to discover the plot on his life through the letters that were given to Rosencrantz and Guildenstern, and how he changed the commission and organised the deaths of his two school friends instead. Osric, who is a silly courtier, enters and informs Hamlet that Laertes has challenged him to a duel. Hamlet accepts and proceeds to confront Laertes and meet the challenge.

Claudius, meanwhile, has put some poison in a large chalice of wine and he has also arranged for Laertes's sword to be tipped with poison, which will cause death when it wounds someone. During the duel Laertes loses his sword, Hamlet picks it up and wounds Laertes with it. Laertes also wounds Hamlet with the poisoned sword, so both men are in mortal danger. Meanwhile, Gertrude drinks to her son from the poisoned chalice, while Claudius stands beside her and does nothing to protect her.

When Laertes realises that he has been fatally wounded and is about to die he repents of his crime and asks forgiveness from Hamlet. Laertes then tells Hamlet about the poisoned chalice and sword and the fact that Claudius is culpable. Hamlet reacts violently by attacking Claudius and killing him with the poisoned sword, while at the same time forcing him to drink from the chalice.

The scene concludes with words from the dying Hamlet, telling Horatio to inform Young Fortinbras that he must take control of the kingship of Denmark. Hamlet also urges Horatio to remain alive and inform the Danish people about the truth. Fortinbras arrives and orders that the body of Hamlet should be carried away like a brave soldier to be buried. The play ends with the death of the leading protagonists—Claudius, Gertrude, Hamlet and Laertes. We also hear that Rosencrantz and Guildenstern are dead because of Hamlet's forgery of the letters.

Questions

1. What is the tone of Hamlet's account of events relating to his sea voyage?
2. (a) What do you think was Laertes's attitude just before he stabbed Hamlet?
   (b) To what extent can it be said that Laertes dies redeemed?
3. Why are Laertes's words, 'the king, the king's to blame' so crucial at this point?
4. Comment on the manner in which (a) Hamlet kills Claudius; and (b) Claudius dies.
5. Why is Hamlet's concern for the succession at the point of death so significant?
6. How do you react to Fortinbras's final comments on Hamlet?

CHARACTER ANALYSIS

HAMLET

Like all Shakespeare's tragic heroes, Hamlet is a very complex character. He has been described as a tardy avenger, an intellectual genius, a procrastinator, a victim of evil circumstances. Many different aspects of his character, both positive and negative, are revealed in the play. Hamlet is a noble and idealistic youth, studying at the university of Wittenberg in Germany, who, when the play opens, has recently lost his father. He is deeply sensitive and clearly loved his father, is endowed with a greatness of mind and possesses an unusual degree of perception and mental agility, qualities that enable him to see through people and master them subtly. We see these qualities in his many soliloquies throughout the play.

When we first meet Hamlet he is dressed totally in black because he is in mourning for his father, who has just been buried. Hamlet is brooding and we see that he treats his uncle Claudius, the new king, in a very negative and cynical manner. It is clear that Hamlet distrusts Claudius and bears a deep hostility towards him. This distrust deepens as the play progresses and we begin to realise that Hamlet trusts very few people. In fact, the only person in whom Hamlet can confide and whom he trusts fully is Horatio, his close friend and fellow scholar at the university. This lack of confidence and distrust in people in the court of Denmark is shown throughout the play, in particular through Hamlet's use of language.

Hamlet finds himself surrounded by lies, falsity, and devious evasions in the court of Denmark. He feels he is living in a world where people everywhere seem to be acting a part. Hamlet does not know who to trust and who, apart from his friend Horatio, he can confide in. So Hamlet begins to use language in a particular way in the play. Language furnishes him with a useful safety valve or defence mechanism: he uses it in order to uncover the truth about other people or to expose the truth about himself, his own motivations and dispositions. In Hamlet's use of language, and his imagery in particular, there is a deliberate intention to cloak his own purposes and intentions and to penetrate through the façade of hypocrisy and falsity that is a hallmark of the palace of Elsinore.

Hamlet is deeply shocked by the fact that his own mother Gertrude has married her husband's brother so soon after the death of her husband. He expresses himself very cynically and very clearly in the image:

... within a month
Ere yet the salt of most unrighteous tears
Had left the flushing in her galled eyes
She married.

Hamlet feels utter shock, disgust and betrayal at his mother's action. Appearance, in her case, has belied reality. Her apparent love for her husband is deeply suspect, since she married Claudius so speedily—within two months of her first husband's death.

When Gertrude reproaches Hamlet for persisting in mourning his father by telling him to:

... cast thy nighted colour off ...
Do not forever with thy veiled lids
Seek for thy noble father in the dust

Hamlet does not take long to reply: 'I have that within which passes show/These but the trappings and the suits of woe.' In other words, Hamlet is outlining vehemently to his own mother that seeming or appearance on the one hand and truth or reality on the other do not always correspond in human nature. He stresses that in her case she needs to take stock and examine her own behaviour.

Hamlet uses language to deal with the corruption and deception that he perceives to be a dominant aspect in the court of Denmark. Most of his exchanges with people like Rosencrantz and Guildenstern, his two old school friends, are filled with a bitter cynicism and innuendo. Claudius invites Rosencrantz and Guildenstern to the palace in order to 'glean' from Hamlet's conversation and behaviour what underlies his mentality and mindset. It soon becomes clear from Hamlet's reactions to his old school pals that he distrusts their motivations totally. From the beginning Hamlet adopts a cautious approach to these two, which is shown in his use of language. When they are not sincere with him about the reason for their arrival at the palace, he chastises them, telling them to 'be even and direct with me whether you were sent for or not'. Of course he eventually gets them to tell him the truth; that they 'were sent for'. Hamlet no longer trusts these two men and as the play unfolds and he realises that they are mere pawns in the hands of the villain Claudius, his disgust and hostility towards them simply intensifies. He calls them 'sponges' that 'soaks up the king's countenances, his rewards, his authorities', and prophetically tells them how Claudius will simply use them for what he has gleaned and then they will be 'dry again'.

Hamlet adopts a similar manner and approach towards Polonius. Polonius is the king's chief counsellor of state and adviser. He is a totally unscrupulous person, who is able to manipulate his own family, particularly Ophelia, and still preach about virtue and good living. Hamlet makes continuous use of language that is made up of misleading statements, innuendoes, illogicalities and ambiguities when he is addressing Polonius in order to show that he despises him and has a complete contempt for his manner of operating.

In the play we are presented with two conflicting views of Hamlet. We see one Hamlet when he is engaged in action and another vision of him when he speaks in soliloquy. When Hamlet uses soliloquy he agonises about his motivations and continuously questions himself about the problems he is facing. Also, in his use of soliloquy we are exposed to a character who is deeply sensitive and has a profound degree of moral awareness and capacity to philosophise. Moreover, many of his soliloquies reveal world-weariness, a deep-seated self-reproach and an undoubted melancholy, all of which seem to be out of proportion with the actual circumstances of life. Some commentators have claimed that Hamlet's active energy seems to be paralysed by an excess of the speculative faculty in his soliloquies. In other words, Hamlet is a very philosophical person who questions many issues in life and feels very deeply about a lot of things.

On the other hand, when Hamlet acts he can be quick-thinking, efficient, businesslike and shrewd. Take, for example, his speedy organisation of the play, 'The Mousetrap', when the players arrive at the palace. He decides to stage a play that evening in order 'to catch the conscience of the king'. He is quick to uncover Claudius's plot to have him killed, and quick to organise the deaths of Rosencrantz and Guildenstern. When he succeeds in exposing Claudius's guilt, Hamlet loses no time in confronting his mother with her guilt and getting her to acknowledge that she has done wrong. All these actions reveal a decisiveness, resolution and promptness of action that is not evident in any of his soliloquies.

There are some less salubrious, or more negative, sides to his character. Many of his soliloquies reveal bitterness, cynicism and melancholy. These characteristics dominate the tone of his exchanges with people like Polonius and Claudius. He also evinces a pagan attitude in his refusal to kill Claudius while he is praying and struggling to repent. Hamlet refrains from killing him because he wants to catch Claudius when he is engaged in actions that have 'no relish of salvation' to them but instead will damn him to hell. We also see undertones of pagan or unchristian sentiments in many of his dealings with his former school friends, Rosencrantz and Guildenstern. He ruthlessly sends them to their death, determined that they will have 'no shriving time', no opportunity to repent. He uses an exceptional degree of verbal violence in the closet scene when he chastises his mother for her guilty behaviour, telling her that she has made 'marriage vows/As false as dicer's oaths' through her alliance with Claudius. Many critics condemn Hamlet's treatment of Ophelia in the Nunnery Scene, when he brutally rejects her and orders her to go to a nunnery, not be a 'breeder of sinners'. His harsh denunciation of her behaviour, the fact that she uses make-up or 'paintings', is particularly cruel. In fact, this scene is exceptionally tragic and cruelly ironic because Hamlet's rejection of Ophelia, and his condemnation of women's frail nature, causes her to have a mental breakdown and subsequently to kill herself.

On the other hand, however, there are many positive features in the representation of Hamlet's character. He possesses an undoubted love for his father and his grief at his father's untimely death is certainly very sincere. Hamlet also has a generous nature that is alien to all types of connivance in evil-doing. Even Claudius acknowledges this fact when he is trying to manipulate Laertes into taking part in a corrupt duel with Hamlet. Claudius tells Laertes how Hamlet will not notice that the foils have been tampered with because he is 'most generous, and free from all contriving/Will not peruse the foils.' Hamlet also possesses a profound and sincere love for the theatre. When the players arrive at Elsinore we see another more relaxed side to Hamlet when he greets them personally and even manages to engage in light banter and jokes.

Another aspect of Hamlet is his popularity with the Danish people, which we learn through Claudius's words: 'He's loved of the distracted multitude.'

As the play develops and the action unfolds, we begin to witness a change in Hamlet's mindset and consequent actions. Shortly before the end of the play, when Hamlet returns from England to Denmark, we hear him speaking to Horatio about how 'There's a divinity that shapes our ends/Rough-hew them how we will.' It is becoming clear that Hamlet now sees his role as avenger in a different light than he had done earlier in the play. Hamlet is now conscious of the fact that he is acting more as an agent of Divine Justice than as an avenger. Of course this notion is quite paradoxical, given the fact that he is speaking about how he has just sent his two old school friends Rosencrantz and Guildenstern to their deaths with 'no shriving time allowed' and all under the sanction of heaven—'even in this was heaven ordinant'.

This new attitude remains with Hamlet right through to the play's conclusion. Hamlet remains confident of the fact that this divinity that shapes our ends will create an opportunity for him to punish Claudius. In fact, his faith is not misplaced. Claudius himself unwittingly provides him with an opportunity by inviting him to engage in a duel with Laertes in the main court of Elsinore.

Hamlet freely embraces the challenge, despite his intuition that things may not be all they seem. He confides in Horatio that he has an uneasy instinct about the challenge, but nonetheless he accepts it. Hamlet seems to be more self-confident about his own ability to take clear, effective action, in contrast to his earlier attempts at unpacking his heart in cynical and satiric words.

We are given the picture of a noble and fine young man in Hamlet in the concluding scenes. We learn how he was likely to have 'proved most royal', when Fortinbras, the newly appointed King of Denmark, enters.

The tribute paid him by his best friend and loyal ally Horatio is perhaps the finest and most fitting conclusion to his career:

Good-night, sweet prince;
And flights of angels sing thee to thy rest.

Hamlet is truly a much-loved prince who possesses a vast degree of human virtue and ability, and whose death is not only tragic but extremely noble.

CLAUDIUS

We first meet Claudius in Act I, Scene ii, when he and his new wife Gertrude are assembled with all the leading counsellors of state in the castle in Elsinore. He explains to them that, while it is justifiable to mourn for his recently deceased brother, the former King of Denmark, it is at the same time justifiable that 'with wisest sorrow' he has now married Gertrude in the interests of the state. Claudius speedily moves on to discuss in more detail the political situation that exists in Denmark. Young Fortinbras from Norway is trying to avenge the death of his father by attempting to regain lands lost by his father to the crown of Denmark. Claudius, a shrewd and deft politician, explains to the court of Denmark how he has decided to send two ambassadors (Voltemand and Cornelius) to Young Fortinbras's uncle in order to suppress the nephew's attempts at war with Denmark.

It is striking that in this scene Claudius succeeds in dominating the whole court with his presence and his words: he conveys a powerful impression of a person totally in control and thoroughly efficient. In fact, this attitude of leadership and efficiency is a fundamental characteristic of his behaviour for much of the play. Claudius is clever and mentally agile, but he is also splendid at dealing with different people. When Laertes requests permission to return to France now that the coronation ceremony is over, Claudius adopts an indulgent tone and even solicits the help of Polonius.

This atmosphere changes, however, when Claudius addresses Hamlet as 'my cousin . . . and my son.' It becomes immediately evident that Hamlet will not be as easy to manipulate as all the others in the court of Denmark. From the outset, Hamlet adopts a bitter and negative tone towards his uncle, telling him, 'I am too much in the sun.' When Gertrude intervenes, telling her son to 'cast thy nighted colour off' and not continue to 'Seek for thy noble father in the dust', Claudius gains courage and chastises Hamlet for his insistence in mourning his dead father. Claudius is anxious to get on with the business of running the state of Denmark and so he leaves shortly afterwards, urging Hamlet to remain in Denmark and not return to Wittenberg. Of course Claudius is shrewd enough to know that it is safer to have Hamlet near him so he can assess all his moves.

Between Claudius's first appearance and his second, in Act II, Scene ii, a lot of things have occurred. Laertes has departed for France. The Ghost has appeared to Hamlet, telling him that Claudius murdered him while he was sleeping in the garden, and instructing him to 'Revenge his foul and most unnatural murder.' It seems that Claudius, in response to the way Hamlet has changed since his father's death, has invited Rosencrantz and Guildenstern, two of Hamlet's old school friends, to stay in the palace and act as spies. Of course, we the audience and reader know that Hamlet has adopted 'an antic disposition' since he heard the truth about his father's death. And this will have affected his relationship with Claudius even more. In fact, Claudius's appearance in this scene enables us to see how successful he is at managing state matters and situations of crisis. Polonius arrives and proceeds to show a letter that Hamlet sent to his daughter, Ophelia, in which he announces that he is dying of love for her. He also tells the king that he cautioned his daughter not to receive any visits from Hamlet and concludes from all this that Hamlet is now suffering from a madness of love after having been rejected by his beloved Ophelia. Claudius is a little more dubious, and the two decide to test the truth of Polonius's theory by organising an encounter between Hamlet and Ophelia, which they will both observe from behind the arras or screen in the hallway of the palace.

It becomes obvious that Claudius feels threatened by Hamlet's presence from the outset of his new reign as King of Denmark. When Hamlet vehemently attacks Ophelia after casually meeting her reading a pious book in the hallway, Claudius realises that he is certainly not suffering from unrequited love: 'Love? His affections do not that way tend.' Claudius is a supreme and skilful opportunist and he immediately decides to get Hamlet out of the way where he will be unable to expose Claudius's villainy to the people of Denmark. There and then, he decides to send him quickly to England, 'For the demand of our neglected tribute', as he realises that 'Madness in great ones must not unwatched go.' With Hamlet out of the way Claudius will be more easily able to manipulate all those others who are blind to his real nature.

Hamlet, however, is one step ahead of this skilful politician. He has organised an entertainment that evening for the royal couple and their entourage in order to prove the authenticity of the Ghost's words and thereby 'catch the conscience' of Claudius.

The outcome of the drama enacted before the court in Elsinore results in a complete success for Hamlet at the same time as giving us another insight into the character of Claudius. When Claudius sees the entire murder enacted before him he jumps up with fright and runs from the room, asking for light. He goes to his small chapel and kneels in prayer before the tabernacle. Earlier, before the Nunnery Scene, when Polonius preached about hypocrisy and how with pious actions we can 'sugar o'er the devil himself', Claudius internally acknowledged the deep burden of his guilt because of his murder. Here, too, in this scene, when Claudius attempts to kneel and repent of his crime, we see another side to him. He is not only the able and clever politician who can manage to avert all crises and dangers, but also a human being conscious of his sins and hungering for forgiveness. Claudius has a conscience that enables him realise that the murder of his own brother is an 'offence' that is 'rank', that 'it smells to heaven,' because 'it hath the primal eldest curse upon't/A brother's murder.'

This scene, which could be called the Prayer Scene, is a fascinating insight into one man's struggles with his conscience and at the same time his lust for power. What is also interesting about this scene and about Claudius's prayer is the graphic insight we are given into his real priorities and the reasons why he carried out the murder in the first place: 'My crown, mine own ambition and my queen.' Gertrude only figures third in his list of priorities.

Meanwhile, the culmination of Claudius's prayer is that he cannot relinquish the fruits of his crime—the throne, along with power and the achievement of his personal ambition. Nor can he give Gertrude up, even though his lust for power seems to be greater than his love for her. Claudius wants the peace that accompanies repentance, but he is not prepared to surrender his kingship.

From this scene (Act III, Scene iii) onwards we witness a profound change in Claudius's mentality and in his language patterns and behaviour. He has abandoned all prospects of forgiveness and he no longer makes any references to guilt, sin and conscience for the remainder of the play. It could even be said that from this stage on, Claudius becomes a ruthless, hardened criminal who slowly immerses himself fully and consciously in evil-doing. From the moment he hears about Polonius's death at the hands of Hamlet, Claudius is bent on protecting himself and getting rid of Hamlet, using whatever means are necessary.

Diseases desperate grown
By desperate appliance are relieved
Or not at all.

This could now sum up Claudius's attitude as he mobilises all the resources in his power to rid himself of Hamlet and the possible threat of exposure.

As the events of this play move towards a conclusion, Claudius finds that 'sorrows come … not single spies/But in battalions.' The return of Laertes offers another threat to Claudius's security. Laertes is popular with the people and his arrival poses one of the most challenging threats to Claudius's reign as monarch. Laertes demands an explanation of his father's death and speedy burial, but Claudius deftly sidesteps his hysterical and hyperbolic reactions, and manages to manipulate the young man into a corrupt duel whose object is the murder of Hamlet with a poisoned rapier. Claudius seems to have a predilection for poison: he murdered his own brother by poisoning him and is now plotting the murder of his nephew by injecting poison into the end of his sword.

Claudius is decisive and opportunistic, unlike his nephew Hamlet. At no stage in the face of the most severe crisis does Claudius lose his nerve. He is characterised throughout by a courteous, dignified and sanguine disposition on every occasion.

Claudius does become a target of the playwright's irony at various stages in this play. When he preaches about the sacred inviolability of kings and the fact that their kingly office protects them by a divine sanction, 'There's such divinity doth hedge a king', we realise that given his track record as a murderous usurper this indeed is real mockery.

At the conclusion of the play Claudius ironically becomes a victim of his own plotting. When Laertes tells Hamlet about the poisoned sword, acknowledging that 'the foul practice/Hath turn'd itself on me', Claudius is then forced to drink from the poisoned chalice. In many ways, Claudius's death is a grim reminder of the self-destructive quality of evil-doing.

It is interesting to examine some of the imagery associated with Claudius throughout this play. The Ghost describes him as 'a serpent', an 'incestuous', 'adulterate beast'. Later on, in the Closet Scene, when Hamlet confronts his mother with the evil nature of her crime in marrying her husband's brother, Claudius is described as 'a mildew'd ear', a 'cutpurse of the empire,' a 'king of shreds and patches'. All these images suggest that he is a man who has become immersed in evil and corruption because he has murdered a lawfully elected king. The bestial images are appropriate in the light of the fact that a character's immersion in moral evil does indeed reduce him or her to the level of a beast.

Claudius is a realistically drawn character who is endowed with a great deal of strength and virtue. He is also invested with a lust for power and a capacity for evil-doing and corruption. In his depiction of the character of Claudius, Shakespeare succeeds in portraying a very rich and vivid picture of a monarch in England in Elizabethan times.

GERTRUDE

It is tragically ironic that so idealistic and morally sensitive an individual as Hamlet should have had Gertrude for his mother. A Laertes would undoubtedly have accommodated himself to such a mother, in a way that Hamlet cannot do. The truth is that Gertrude must be seen as a rather too 'merry widow', a figure appropriate to a bedroom comedy or farce, a woman still voluptuously beautiful, aware of herself as a woman, instinctively flirtatious, even with her son—'Come hither my dear Hamlet, sit by me'—a woman who has not learned how to grow old gracefully, for lust still 'mutine[s] in a matron's bones'. She is evidently the type of woman who cannot do without a man.

In describing his mother's love of his father during the latter's lifetime, Hamlet significantly uses terms suggestive of the animal and the fleshly—the emphasis is not on the emotional but on the physical and the sensuous:

> Why, she would hang on him
> As if increase of appetite had grown
> By what it fed on.

Hamlet's attitude towards the marriage of his mother and father had been that of the typical idealistic adolescent. He had seen his mother and father as ideal types and their marriage as a remote, unassailable perfection. Tragically, however, the 'heyday' in Gertrude's blood was far from 'tame', and even in her husband's lifetime her sensual weakness had succumbed to the 'witchcraft' of Claudius's wit, so that the 'seeming virtuous' queen had become an adulteress, even before she entered into an incestuous marriage with her husband's brother after the former's death.

It is this indecently hasty and unnatural union of his mother and his uncle that makes Hamlet feel that life is merely an 'unweeded garden', possessed only of 'things rank and gross in nature'. His vision of the world is irrevocably darkened, he sees all women from henceforth as potential betrayers: 'Frailty, thy name is woman', even before the Ghost's revelation of Gertrude's adultery.

The easy banality of his mother's advice to Hamlet to 'cast thy nighted colour off' and her pleas to her son to come to terms with his father's death—

> Thou knowest 'tis common—all that lives must die
> Passing through nature to eternity

—seem to Hamlet the most monstrous of rationalisations. He relates her words back to her own easy show of grief, when she followed her husband's corpse to the grave 'like Niobe, all tears', a grief without depth or reality, since it was the mere perfunctory prelude to her 'posting' with indecent haste towards her perverted union with her second husband. Hamlet castigates Gertrude for her hypocrisy; her grief was mere 'seeming':

> These indeed seem
> For they are actions that a man might play.

Gertrude then becomes, in her son's eyes, a 'Player Queen'. Her brief mourning for her dead husband was a matter merely of assuming 'the trappings and the suits of woe'.

From the very outset, therefore, Gertrude is part of the 'rottenness' at the heart of things in Denmark. She can pose decorously as the 'Imperial jointress of the State', taken to wife by the newly elected King of Denmark Claudius for reasons of state, but the truth about her position is uglier. Sly, superficial and amoral as she is, Gertrude fits quite easily into the world of 'seeming' created by Claudius. She is at home in the brilliant materialistic microcosm of Elsinore with its frenetic lust for life, its emphasis on the here and now, its debased value systems, its acceptance of the status quo, its desire to 'bear all smooth and even', and its delight in the pleasures of the senses.

In her flaccid fashion, she loves her son, and is concerned and uneasy about his state of mind, which she is shrewd enough to relate to 'our overhasty marriage'. Hamlet's outraged moral sensitivity she sees merely as awkward Puritanism—no doubt she hopes he will outgrow it and come eventually to 'look like a friend on Denmark'—in other words on his stepfather.

She is as eager as Claudius to have Rosencrantz and Guildenstern, Hamlet's former school friends 'lead on to pleasures' because of her 'too much changed son'. No doubt Gertrude, like Claudius, would have wished that her son could have been another Laertes, eager to take his 'fair hour' in sowing his harmless wild oats, the prerogative of thoughtless youth. Instead she must contend with a son who is brooding, alien and an increasingly dangerous presence at court, a son who is a constant reproach to herself and an obvious enemy of her husband. Hamlet has become for her a son who appears to have been driven mad as a result of her own behaviour.

Gertrude's tragedy lies in her moral myopia. As one critic suggests, the tragedy hinges on her 'not noticing and not understanding'. Her vision is fleshly and physical, confined to the material, her reason founded on the senses and essentially downward looking. Of the earth, and earthy, Gertrude cannot deal with anything other than the events of this world.

Thus, in the closet episode, when Hamlet confronts her with what he sees as her part in his father's and his own betrayal and tells her of his father's visitations, it is significant that Gertrude cannot see the spirit. She sees the material world, 'all that is', and nothing beyond it. The tragedy in this brief domestic interlude lies in the irrevocable severing of husband and son from the woman whose attenuated moral vision has led her to betray both of them. It is not until this particular episode, the Closet Scene, Act III, Scene iv, that Gertrude comes to an understanding of what has been her position. Only now does she take an intrinsic interest in her own plight. Her unfeigned horror at the suggestion conveyed in Hamlet's accusation, 'A bloody deed—almost as bad, good mother/As kill a king, and marry with his brother', makes clear her innocence of complicity in Claudius's murder of her first husband. As the interview proceeds, however, Gertrude begins to see herself with new and horrified eyes. At first she reacts with a sense of justified outrage. Her son has behaved abominably—he has 'his father much offended'. She becomes angry when Hamlet retorts that it is she who has offended his father. Then his wild words and manner begin to alarm her—in her eyes, he is, after all, mad. 'Thou wilt not murther me?' she asks in terror, when he flings her back into a chair and talks about setting up 'a glass/Wherein you may see the inmost part of you'. Mindful of Polonius behind the arras, she calls for help, only to have the eavesdropper killed in her presence.

Gertrude is so thoroughly a part of Claudius's world that at first she can make little of what her son says. What does he mean by his wild talk of an 'act that blurs the grace and blush of modesty;/Calls virtue hypocrite', turns 'sweet religion' into 'a rhapsody of words'? His intellectualised generalisations mean nothing to his shallow-minded mother. Hamlet proceeds to produce two pictures, the 'counterfeit presentment' of the dead king and his living brother, and manages to make her see the truth behind her own preference for Claudius, the pseudo king and satyr, over Hamlet, the real king and godlike man. She has taken appearance for reality, has left the 'fair mountain' to 'batten on this moor'. What she calls love is merely lust. As Hamlet describes Gertrude's relationships with Claudius in ever grosser images, he finally wears her down, so that she comes to see herself through his outraged eyes.

O Hamlet, speak no more!
Thou turns't mine eyes into my very soul
And there I see such black and grained spots
As will not leave their tinct.

From now on Gertrude is a woman adrift. She has now become aware of her own guilt, and has gained a new insight into the real nature of the man who is her husband, and so she tells Hamlet that her heart is cleft in twain. She listens in meek submission now to what her son has to say and asks with bewildered uncertainty 'What shall I do?', promising finally not to reveal what has passed between them:

> Be thou assured, if words be made of breath
> And breath of life, I have no life to breathe
> What thou hast said to me.

Hamlet's interview with Gertrude here in the Closet Scene is undoubtedly a climactic turning point in the play. The exchange between mother and son has about it an extraordinary intensity and urgency. All of Hamlet's long pent-up anger and outrage is released in a great flood-tide of passionate expression and action.

After the long and harrowing interview with her son, Gertrude moves into the shadows, no longer a focal point in the drama. She appears with Claudius in the subsequent court scenes, but says little and seems removed from much of the action around her. She seeks to disarm criticism of Hamlet, by using his madness to excuse him, and she appears to have withdrawn from Claudius, though this is merely hinted at in the subsequent scenes. In a significant aside in Act IV, Scene v she refers to her 'sick soul' and to sin's 'true nature', suggesting a deep and settled depressive condition. In her sensitive and moving account of Ophelia's death and her sad comment as she strews flowers over the grave later, there is perhaps further evidence that Hamlet's admonitions have had their effect on her better nature.

She dies with a strong sense of poetic justice, as a result of her husband's failure to save her. Claudius loved Gertrude, his 'mouse' as he called her, in his fashion, but his instinct for survival was stronger than his feelings for his wife. When he saw her lift the poisoned cup to her lips he moved instinctively to prevent her from drinking its contents, but then, aware that he would betray himself if he intervened, held back in guilty silence. Gertrude's death goes almost unnoticed by the audience, whose eyes are focused on the final clash of 'mighty opposites', Hamlet and Claudius. Tragically, Gertrude's epitaph is a mere cursory afterthought on Hamlet's part: 'Wretched queen, adieu'.

Even though she is a weak and uninteresting character, Gertrude is important for a number of reasons.
- She is, of course, as 'Player Queen', central to the play's concern with appearance and reality.
- She is part of Denmark's world of 'seeming', the world of false appearances with which

the hero has to contend.

- In her moral obtuseness, she is an integral aspect of the moral topsy-turvy value system operative in that world
- She is Hamlet's mother and our chief interest in her derives from our interest in him.

OPHELIA

Ophelia is the daughter of Polonius, the chief counsellor of state to the King of Denmark. When we first meet her we learn that both her father and her brother, Laertes, treat her as a vulnerable and weak person, a 'green girl', who seems not to have a mind of her own.

She is a young and inexperienced girl who shows herself to be obedient to both her father and brother. It becomes clear that Ophelia has lived a sheltered life and grew up in a household of dominant and aggressive males. Both these men, Polonius and Laertes, make efforts to protect this vulnerable and innocent girl from the predatory sexuality they suspect in Hamlet. They both warn her, in different ways and at different times, to lock herself away from Hamlet's predatory advances.

It would appear from the play that Hamlet did love Ophelia very much. He tells her this in the Nunnery Scene and also reveals it in the Graveyard Scene. The really interesting question here is *why* Hamlet should have chosen to single out a girl like Ophelia, who in her youthful innocence and inexperience must have seemed out of place among the sophisticated, worldly wise courtiers of Elsinore. Polonius reminds us that it is 'of late' that Hamlet had begun to pay court to his daughter. Perhaps he singled her out simply because she had not acquired the colouring of that court world. Perhaps he chose her because she is at a polar extreme from the experienced sensualist Gertrude. Perhaps he turned from the corrupt world of 'seeming', where Gertrude is at home, with its all too real and obtrusive basis in carnality, to find relief in the innocent idealism of a boy and girl romance with Ophelia. This was certainly how *she* saw it:

> The courtier's, scholar's, soldier's eye, tongue, sword, the observed of all observers . . .
> And I of ladies most deject and wretched
> That suck'd the music of his honey vows . . .
> To have seen what I have seen, see what I see.

Tragically, however, the relationship between these two people is doomed to failure in the corrupt world of the Elsinore court. Ophelia, in her innocence and vulnerability, becomes nothing more than a tragic pawn in the dangerous games being played out by people of whose nature she is quite ignorant. Exploited in turn by Hamlet and Polonius, she becomes progressively more bewildered, more disoriented and more isolated.

As the plot develops and the action unfolds, Ophelia becomes an example of one whose sufferings are disproportionate to her original offences. She clearly loves Hamlet and experiences a profound degree of suffering when he rejects her in the Nunnery Scene, telling her to get to a nunnery and not to breed sinners.

In many ways Ophelia is the antithesis of Gertrude. Ophelia is an innocent. She is virtuous, even though to Hamlet she seems not to be. In Act III, Scene i, Polonius gives her a pious book to read in order to use her as a pawn so that he and Claudius may glean more about Hamlet's motivations and mindset. And so Hamlet finds her in the corridor looking the model of virtue and innocence. He soon understands that her innocence is being used against him, and so denounces the falsity of womanhood in strong, vehement language. Yet ironically Ophelia is an innocent. Despite Hamlet's cruelty towards her, and the fact that her father manipulates her, Ophelia remains a constant lover. Tragically, Ophelia is forced to play a role forced on her by her corrupt and unscrupulous father and to reject the man she loves, only to find herself violently rejected by him.

Ophelia becomes a victim of selfishness and manipulation. She falls victim to the corruption of Polonius and Claudius, and later we see her as a victim of Hamlet's disgust with women, which originates from Gertrude's character and her failure as a mother figure. It was Gertrude's crime that took off

> the rose
> From the fair forehead of an innocent love,
> And set a blister there.

The 'innocent love' could refer to that between Hamlet and Ophelia. The blister is the incest, and maybe even Hamlet's obscene taunting in the Nunnery Scene. Ironically, Ophelia's innocence contributes to destroying her in the play.

Ophelia's role, then, is as crucial and as complex as Gertrude's. Her innocence and idealism acts as a counterbalance to Gertrude's earthly carnality. Her love might have been Hamlet's saving grace, but her failure to stand up to her father is a form of betrayal of Hamlet.

Hamlet's approach to Ophelia darkens, as she allows herself to become the decoy in Polonius's ugly little intrigue. In this episode he sees her as a prostitute 'loosed' to a client. This is what Polonius has done, but also what she has allowed to be done to herself. Hence the searing irony of the 'Get thee to a nunnery' speech, provoked not only by the falsity of Ophelia's own behaviour, but by the parallel it presents for Hamlet with the behaviour of his mother: 'I have heard of your paintings too . . .'

There is a further aspect to this 'nunnery' episode, which heightens the interest for a contemporary audience. In the original story on which this play was based, Ophelia's equivalent was a prostitute, intended to trap Hamlet, even though she fell in love with him. Shakespeare retains her role as the decoy, but he transforms the character into the simple, virtuous, sheltered girl we encounter in his version of the story. It is this background detail that lends such complexity to Hamlet's angry adjuration 'Get thee to a nunnery', since 'nunnery' was common slang for 'brothel' in Shakespeare's time.

We can see therefore that for Hamlet women are either prostitutes or destined to become prostitutes—and thus betrayers of men: 'men know well enough what monsters you make of them.' Hamlet wants Ophelia to go to a nunnery before she betrays more men. Throughout the Nunnery Scene, Ophelia is involved in the theme of 'seeming', which is so central to this drama. Through her false role-playing she becomes a part of that corrupt world of Elsinore where 'seeming' is the norm, yet remains virtuous herself.

Ophelia's madness too is related to a central theme of the play. Her real madness contrasts with Hamlet's assumed lunacy and is a reminder to the audience how both people have reacted to shocking and traumatic events in their lives. Ophelia, like Hamlet, finds herself in a world of evil—a world where her lover goes mad and kills her father, while at the same time brutally rejecting her. Tragically her end seems to have been suicide.

Ophelia becomes a dramatic symbol of the inadequacy of innocence in a world dominated by corruption at its heart. The use of spring imagery in the representation of her character is intended to highlight her tragic frailty, as well as the beauty of that youthful idealism and innocence that she embodies:

> And from her fair and unpolluted flesh
> May violets spring.

It is appropriate in its own ironic fashion that it is Gertrude who gives the news of Ophelia's death in language and images we would not have expected of her: 'in the glassy stream . . . fantastic garlands did she make of crowflowers, nettles, daisies and long purples . . .' It would appear that Gertrude has begun to recognise that Ophelia was an innocent victim of circumstances beyond her control.

THE GHOST

The Ghost is the catalyst of the play's action, triggering the plot by disclosing the details of his murder at the hands of the present King of Denmark, Claudius.

Despite the fact that the Ghost makes only three appearances on stage, his presence and the fears and doubts about the 'world' from which he came are never far from the overt concerns of the play's hero. Hamlet has seen his father's 'disturbed spirit', and is aware that the 'poor ghost' suffers for sins done 'in his state of nature'.

Hamlet's concern with the manner of his father's death, with the fact that Claudius had sent his brother into the afterlife, 'no shriving time allowed', and with the Ghost's own horror at his unexpected death, not only underlines the Christian thinking behind the play, but more significantly becomes the son's rationale for sparing Claudius while the latter is at prayer:

> He took my father grossly, full of bread
> With all his crimes broad blown, as flush as May
> And how his audit stands, who knows, save heaven?
> But in our circumstance and course of thought
> 'Tis heavy with him; and am I then revenged,
> To take him in the purging of his soul
> When he is fit and seasoned for his passage?

He determines to await the perfection of revenge, to catch Claudius in some act that 'hath no relish of salvation in it', so that the latter's soul may be irrevocably damned. Later, he says that he 'waits on the king's pleasure'. He adds, 'If his fitness speaks, mine is ready': he is obviously referring again to Claudius's 'fitness' not simply for death, but for damnation. In this context, it is noteworthy that the newly hardened Hamlet sends Claudius's stool pigeons, Rosencrantz and Guildenstern, to a similar end.

We must remember that the Ghost's role is *many-sided*. We are reminded constantly in this play of the living past of the Ghost (Hamlet's father), and his qualities as a king, a father, a husband and a brother. The Ghost is constantly referred to in terms of an unapproachable ideal: he was the effectively active monarch who defeated the elder Fortinbras and fought against the 'sledded Polacks on the ice'. He is the 'wholesome ear' that is blasted by the 'mildew'd' Claudius. He is also the loving and tender husband who 'might not beteem the winds of heaven' to blow too roughly on Gertrude's check. He is the father idolised by the son, to a perhaps dangerous degree, a father felt by that son to be as unlike him as Hamlet feels himself to be unlike Hercules, the strong man and hero of myth.

Hamlet's idolisation of his father is in fact one of the central, implicit problems of the play, and perhaps one of the reasons behind his delay. His comment to Horatio on the subject of his father is tragically revealing:

> He was a man, take him for all in all;
> I shall not look upon his like again.

Burdened by his own sense of inferiority to his father, uncertain of his identity in a world from which all certainties have disappeared, Hamlet drifts rudderless and paralysed for much of the play. His father's death and the manner of it, coupled with his mother's infidelity, have combined to destroy Hamlet's vision of the world, as he thought he knew it: he has become, even at our first introduction to him, and before he has learned the worst from the Ghost, an Adam unparadised.

Central to an analysis of the Ghost's place in the drama is the problem presented by his nature. Shakespeare has left the identity of the Ghost deliberately ambiguous in order to lend weight to Hamlet's own doubts concerning the spirit. In Shakespeare's day there were conflicting views as to the nature of spirits from that 'undiscovered country, from whose bourne/No traveller returns'. Certain Protestant sects, rejecting the concept of purgatory, were convinced that supernatural 'materialisations' were inevitably either angelic or diabolical. This latter belief would be confirmed in the fears expressed by both Horatio and Hamlet that the Ghost is a 'goblin damned', who has appeared to Hamlet in order to bring about his damnation: it 'abuses me to damn me'.

However, ancient Catholic traditions lingered on in post-Reformation England, and the Ghost's revelations do suggest a purgatorial background: he is confined

> for a certain term ... to fast in fires
> Till the foul crimes, done in my days of nature
> Are burnt and purged away ...

It was commonly believed, even by pious Protestants, that ghosts revisited the earth as a warning to the living, to right wrongs done during their lifetimes, to reveal the location of hidden treasure or the fact of a hidden crime. This belief fits in well enough with Shakespeare's Ghost in *Hamlet* and with what is said of the reason for its appearance: 'This bodes some strange eruption to our state'; 'There's something rotten in the state of Denmark'; 'My father's spirit in arms! All is not well; /I doubt some foul play'; 'If thou art privy to thy country's fate/Which, happily, foreknowing may avoid,/O, speak.'

One critic has aptly made the point concerning Shakespeare's Ghost that anyone, Catholic, Protestant or Dissenter, attending the play would have found in Shakespeare's portrayal of Hamlet's dead father confirmation of their own beliefs concerning the spirit world.

That there *was* a Ghost, that the 'thing' apparently seen by the soldiers and by Hamlet was neither a product of the ignorance and superstition of simple men on the one hand, nor of the overheated imagination and grief-stricken emotion of the prince on the other, is attested to by Horatio's reaction. Horatio represents Renaissance scepticism and empiricism on this issue, and Shakespeare uses him to convince us about the 'reality' of the Ghost. His stoutly held scepticism—'Horatio says 'tis but our fantasy'; 'Tush, tush, 'twill not appear'— is subjected to an almost comic reversal at sight of the apparition:

> Before my God, I might not this believe, without the sensible and true avouch
> Of mine own eyes.

Later he confirms the truth of what he has seen to Hamlet: 'I knew your father;/These hands are not more like'. The Ghost, then, is not a hallucinatory image, not the product of delusion: it is to be taken seriously as a metaphysical reality.

There is still, however, the puzzle of the Ghost's nature, its identity. Some contemporary critics suggest that Shakespeare intended his audience to see the Ghost as a sinister figure bringing death and turmoil to the world of Elsinore, winning Hamlet's trust by revealing a truth, but only in order to lead the hero to personal destruction and the destruction of others. Undoubtedly, some support may be found in the text for such an interpretation. Hamlet himself dallies with the thought that the spirit he has seen 'may be the devil', a 'goblin damned' rather than a 'spirit of health'. He knows that the Devil has power 't'assume a pleasing shape' and is potent in cases of melancholic depression such as Hamlet's. His own attitude to the Ghost in Act I, Scene v appears to range from absolute conviction, while he is in the presence of the spirit, to a peculiar hysterical levity, more in keeping with a view of the Ghost as devil, after the Ghost's stage 'disappearance': 'Ah, ha, boy! Says't thou so? Art thou there, truepenny? Come on—you hear this fellow in the cellarage.'

On the other hand, this peculiar contradiction on Hamlet's part can easily be explained in terms of his own unbalanced state of mind, and he reverts to his former respectful tone in his final farewell to the Ghost: 'Rest, rest, perturbed spirit.' Again, in contemplating the horror of the Ghost's revelation, Hamlet invokes heaven and almost instinctively adds 'shall

I couple hell?', appearing here to question the Ghost's origin, but at once he reproaches himself: 'O fie'.

We hear no more of Hamlet's doubts until he voices them once more in connection with his project to catch the conscience of the king though miming the latter's crime in 'The Murder of Gonzago'. Shakespeare leaves it up to us to decide just how important a factor in Hamlet's delay was his uncertainty as to the nature of the Ghost.

The Ghost's third appearance is significant. It occurs after the play within a play scene, after Hamlet has declared to Horatio that he will 'take the Ghost's word for a thousand pound', and after Hamlet has failed to make the most of his opportunity on that occasion and has spared Claudius at prayer. Hamlet suffers doubts as to the Ghost's identity on this occasion and anticipates the latter's reproach: 'Hast thou not come thy tardy son to chide?'

The Ghost on this occasion is very different from the awe-inspiring figure of Act I, and this time his visit could almost be described as a domestic intrusion. In this scene we witness the meeting between the dead husband and father, the son, and the mother and wife. The Ghost's tone is different; he comes only to whet his son's almost blunted purpose and to intervene on Gertrude's behalf. His 'Do not forget' contrasts with the earlier imperious 'Remember me.' Significantly, Gertrude fails to see her husband on this occasion, either because of her innate moral insensitivity, her essential 'worldliness', or because she was unfaithful to him in life. Instead, with a bitter twist of irony, she is confirmed, if only temporarily, in her comforting belief that her son is indeed out of his mind. No wonder Hamlet reacts with a horror that borders on despair as he begs her, 'lay not that flattering unction to your soul'—that it is his madness that accounts for what he has been saying to her. Never before has the radical nature of the differences between the mindsets of son and mother been so sharply emphasised as it is here in the presence of the Ghost, who was husband to one and father to the other.

Hamlet's attitude to the Ghost on this occasion is also different from his earlier approach in Act I. Now he seems less afraid, less in awe of the spirit and more compassionate.

> Do not look on me
> Lest with this piteous action you convert my stern affects.

There is even a suggestion of conflict here between father and son on the subject of the queen. The Ghost's appearance, it is implied, has been occasioned by the son's having allowed himself to be deflected from his original purpose and by his active disobedience in allowing his mind to 'contrive against his mother'. The son has not left his mother to find her own way to repentance, but has felt the need 'to catch her conscience' as well as that of the king. The husband's tender protectiveness of his wife in life has clearly continued in death, and now he intervenes to spare her further suffering, pleading with his son to 'come between her and her fighting soul', because, as he reminds Hamlet, 'conceit in weakest natures strongest works'. Soon afterwards, Hamlet sees his father's spirit 'steal away'. This is a very different kind of departure from the martial stalking off that marked the Ghost's earlier manifestations.

The Ghost does not appear again, neither does Hamlet ever again refer to him in his character as spirit visitant. Yet we cannot doubt that Hamlet continues to brood upon the Ghost and his revelations.

In considering the nature of the Ghost we must allow that there is certain ambivalence in his portrayal. He is, for example, fiercely vindictive in referring to Claudius as 'that incestuous, that adulterate beast'. This personal hatred seems out of keeping both with the character of a 'saved soul' from purgatory and with a dead king intent on righting Claudius's wrong.

Again, the Ghost appears somewhat complacent in preferring his own 'gifts' to those of Claudius. It is one of the cruel paradoxes of this play that the 'casual slaughters', 'deaths put on by cunning and forced cause' and 'purposes mistook' that characterise the events towards the play's conclusion could be seen as the consequences of a divinely authorised visitation by one who comes to set right Denmark's 'disjointed time'. The Ghost's revelations, it cannot be denied, do indeed set in motion a train of dire events and cruel circumstances involving guilty and innocent people alike.

While it may be tempting to read *Hamlet* as a tragedy of damnation, with the Ghost as evil genius and Hamlet as victim of his malign promptings, such an interpretation is misguided. The feeling of the play runs counter to such a reading. Despite his doubts and the riddles concerning his delay, there is little doubt that Hamlet himself sees his revenge in terms of a sense of filial and princely duty.

One feature of the Ghost's commands makes it appear unlikely that Shakespeare intended us to think of him as an evil spirit. During his earthly life he suffered bitter wrong at Gertrude's hands, yet it would appear that the loving tenderness and concern for his queen has continued in the afterlife. Apart from the sad acknowledgement of her betrayal, the Ghost shows an admirable spirit of forbearance towards his faithless and fickle wife. He is emphatic in his injunction to Hamlet,

Taint not thy mind, nor let thy soul contrive
Against thy mother aught.

She is to be left to 'heaven' and to 'the thorns that in her bosom lodge/To prick and sting her'. Later, in the Closet Scene, it is precisely because Hamlet has disobeyed the Ghost's injunctions, has run counter to the Ghost's projected plan for him, that the Ghost returns to intervene on Gertrude's behalf:

> But look, amazement on thy mother sits;
> O, step between her and her fighting soul . . .

Perhaps he senses a grace in her that Hamlet cannot see, or perhaps he remains the doting husband, even as Ghost. In either case these are not the sentiments of a 'goblin damned'.

To conclude, the Ghost:

- appears three times in the play
- is presented in an ambivalent manner
- is the catalyst of the play's action
- has many aspects to his character and figure
- represents the world of the supernatural.

POLONIUS

Polonius is the principal counsellor of state in Denmark. He operates as the king's right-hand man, following his directions at every stage in the play's development. We first meet him in the palace of Elsinore during the coronation ceremony in Act I, Scene ii. We realise at once that he is very long-winded in his speeches and use of words. Polonius and his two children, Laertes and Ophelia, inhabit the subplot of this play.

It would appear, from his manner of speaking and from Hamlet's many comments about 'old men', that Polonius is an old man, bordering almost on dotage. The fact that he is a chief adviser to the king is meant to demonstrate that he is still held in respect in relation to court life and the intrigue and politics associated with it. He certainly possesses a number of qualities that enable him to carry out this fairly prestigious political position. Polonius is valued by Claudius as a useful functionary.

However, there are many different pictures given to us of Polonius in this play. Claudius describes him as a man who is 'faithful and honourable', while Hamlet simply writes him off as a 'wretched, rash, intruding fool', and Gertrude refers to him as 'the unseen, good, old man'.

It is important to evaluate which of these different estimations of Polonius's character are in fact true.

In all his speeches Polonius adopts a long-winded and moralising tone which in many ways seems to be designed to indicate to people that he is wise and something of a sage. This attempt at wisdom and sagacity are very quickly dispelled every time Hamlet encounters him in the play. In fact, Polonius often becomes a target for Hamlet's ironic and satiric attacks, which seem designed to uncover Polonius's deviousness and lies. Even Gertrude chastises him at one stage for his use of windy rhetoric and ramblings in her terse reprimand, 'More matter, with less art.'

Polonius is forgetful. In Act II, Scene i, in the middle of a speech to Reynaldo about spying on his own son, he loses track of what he is saying:

> And then sir, does he this,—he does—
> what was I about to say? By the mass, I was about to
> say something: Where did I leave?

Shakespeare seems to make use of many such instances in the play to mock this man who thinks of himself with a great deal of haughty arrogance and smugness. Take, for example, when he informs the court about the nature of Hamlet's madness:

> Hath there been such a time . . .
> That I have positively said ''Tis so,'
> When it proved otherwise?

This sense of smug self-confidence also governs his relations with his own children. He smothers Laertes in a blanket of moral advice before he embarks for France. Many of these pieces of advice, while wise in themselves, also highlight Polonius's genuine capacity for self-interest and self-love.

Yet at the same time Polonius is undoubtedly a family man who manifests a concern for the best interests of his two children. This concern, however, has different manifestations, some of which are morally reprehensible. For example, he decides to send a servant to spy on his own son while he is in France. Indeed, the manner in which the servant is instructed to do this would certainly imply that Polonius is far from an honourable man:

> Your bait of falsehood take this carp of truth . . .
> By indirections find directions out.

There are also indications that this man's sense of morality is quite seriously retarded when shortly afterwards he has no scruples about sacrificing his daughter's integrity and honour in the interests of the king. Polonius's attempts to use Ophelia to trap Hamlet highlights his unscrupulous nature, and it is not surprising that shortly afterwards Hamlet describes him as Jephthah (a corrupt figure from the Bible).

Another negative aspect of Polonius's character is that he has so little respect for people's personal freedom. He has no qualms about sending a servant to spy on his own son or about exposing his daughter's letters before the whole Danish court. Nor does he seem to be too concerned about using his daughter as a dupe in order to further the king's corrupt intentions. When Hamlet goes to confront his mother with his knowledge of her guilt, Polonius is already in her room, spying on the conversation and determined to tell Claudius everything. Ironically, as he goes to hide behind the curtain in her room, he tells her how 'I'll silence me even here.' These are his last words in the play: he is rendered truly silent when he is slain by Hamlet shortly afterwards. It could be seen as fully appropriate that Polonius is killed in an act of spying, since this was a hallmark of his behaviour throughout the drama.

In conclusion, Polonius is certainly a more complex character than he appears. He has far more shades than either the king or queen he serves. There is a warmth and love—though misguided at times—between him and his children. Ophelia's madness and suicide, and Laertes's vengeful wrath, highlight their genuine affection for their father. He can also be seen as a long-standing and loyal vassal of the state who has faithfully served his king, and as such has the welfare of the state in mind.

However, many of his actions are not only cynical and insincere, but truly corrupt. In many ways Polonius can be seen as a symbol of the corruption that 'is rotten in the state' of Denmark. Polonius has allied himself to a king whose position was earned through murder and deception, and however many virtues he may possess, it cannot be denied that serving a corrupt monarch intensifies many of his own evil traits in the play. Tragically, Polonius too becomes a victim of Claudius's poisonous rule.

HORATIO

Horatio is a friend of Hamlet who is described as a 'scholar'. He is obviously studying in the university of Wittenberg with Hamlet. Horatio has quite an important part in the play insofar as he seems to be the only person in Denmark whom Hamlet can trust. So Horatio's primary importance lies in his relationship with Hamlet. Initially, when he hears about the Ghost he is sceptical about its existence, but this changes very soon. Horatio's judgments seem to be the ones that Hamlet can rely on in a world where he finds himself surrounded by deviousness and lies.

Horatio possesses many positive virtues. He is a man of honour and integrity. This becomes evident from the play's outset, when the guards treat him with respect and reverence as they tell him about their encounter with the Ghost. Hamlet's first meeting with Horatio is undoubtedly filled with a great deal of sincere and heartfelt warmth: 'I am glad to see you well/Horatio.'

Horatio is a very good listener and a man who observes things silently. It is clear that many people, and especially Hamlet, are led to confide in him and respect his opinion. In fact, Horatio is used in this play as a man whom Hamlet finds distinctly different in many ways from himself. At one stage shortly before the commencement of 'The Mousetrap' play, Hamlet is carried away by his praise for Horatio, telling him that 'blest are those/ Whose blood and judgment are so well commeddled/That they are not a pipe for Fortune's finger/ To sound what stop she please.' Give me that man, Hamlet prays, 'That is not passion's slave, and I will wear him/In my heart's core, ay in my heart of heart.' Perhaps there is a suggestion here that Hamlet is lamenting the lack of these virtues and qualities within himself. It would seem that in this Danish court of false seeming and role playing Horatio is the only authentic figure who is true to himself, a man of the utmost integrity and virtue.

Horatio is a man who is loyal to the end. When Ophelia falls victim to mad ramblings it is Horatio who manifests a deep concern for her welfare by telling the queen, ''Twere good she were spoken with; for she may strew/ Dangerous conjectures in ill-breeding minds.'

During 'The Mousetrap', when Hamlet is testing the truth about the Ghost, Hamlet uses Horatio to help him assess Claudius's guilt. When Hamlet has successfully caught 'the conscience of the king', we again see how Horatio is used to mirror Hamlet's excited and ecstatic responses.

Horatio's role in Act V becomes much more significant, and he is on the stage for most of the act. He is the first to hear the news about Hamlet's return to Denmark. He receives a letter informing him where Hamlet is hiding: 'These good fellows will bring you where I am.' Throughout the Graveyard Scene, Horatio is beside Hamlet while the latter engages in many philosophical speculations about death, life after death and the fate of corrupt monarchs. It would seem that Horatio is used as a vehicle through which Hamlet can articulate ideas that he would not otherwise be able to express. It is in his conversation with Horatio that we learn about the fate of Rosencrantz and Guildenstern and how they have been sent to their deaths in England with 'no shriving time allowed'. We also learn how Hamlet's attitude towards revenge has changed somewhat since his return to Denmark. Hamlet feels now that there is a 'special divinity in the fall of a sparrow', that there is an inevitable pattern about events in life that he will follow with peace of mind.

His attitude to death is different now. He feels that death is inevitable and he is ready to face it when and in whatever way it comes: 'If it be now, 'tis not to come; if it be not to come, it will be now; if it be not now, yet it will come: the readiness is all.' It is interesting that all these conversations take place in the presence of his true and only friend, Horatio. When Hamlet is wounded with the poisoned sword, Horatio is by his side immediately, willing to take the same road by drinking from the poisoned chalice in order to be united in death with his friend. But Hamlet urges Horatio—the only honest man— to stay alive so that the truth will be vindicated and given its rightful place and hearing.

As Hamlet dies it is Horatio who speaks the words that form a fitting epitaph:

> Good-night, sweet prince;
> And flights of angels sing thee to thy rest.

It is also Horatio who sums up the essence of what this play has been about:

> Of carnal, bloody and unnatural acts
> Of accidental judgments, casual slaughters;
> Of deaths put on by cunning and forc'd cause.

Horatio commands a position on centre stage as the events of this tragedy come to their conclusion.

Horatio has several functions in this play. He is the man of honesty and loyalty, the man who vindicates the truth and pays homage to his friend. In a world saturated with deception, dissimulation and lies, Horatio stands upright and at odds with those who propagate evil and corruption; he is the antithesis of many of the main characters in this play. He is also used as a sounding board or figure through which the audience can gain insights into the mindset and motivations of the central protagonist, Hamlet.

LAERTES

Laertes can be seen as a foil of Hamlet. He is the son of Polonius, the chief counsellor of state in the court of Denmark.

Laertes can be viewed not only in his role as avenger but also in the way he operates in his own family. Here Shakespeare draws some subtle and significant contrasts. Polonius is a far from ideal father, yet the family he heads is a far less dysfunctional one than Hamlet's, with his 'uncle-father and aunt-mother'; and while Laertes was allowed to 'take his fair hour' and return to France, to continue living in semi-independence while he sowed his wild oats, Hamlet is forced to remain in the Denmark that has become a prison to him.

Laertes may be worldly wise, cynical and sophisticated, but he possesses some appealing qualities in relation to his sister Ophelia. He talks to her and speaks of her with an intimate fondness and even a certain lyrical reverence, using imagery of flowers and of spring to suggest his sense of her virginal quality and of the ideal, innocent character of her love: 'O Rose of May'; 'And from her fair and unpolluted flesh/May violets spring'; 'A violet in the youth of primy nature'; 'The canker galls the infants of the spring'. Laertes is genuinely protective of Ophelia.

Laertes may be criticised for his sensational and histrionic show of grief in the graveyard when Ophelia is being buried. Yet when Hamlet appears he is ready to forgive Laertes for the 'bravery' of his expression of sorrow at the graveside because Hamlet is deeply aware of the fact that both are experiencing deep sorrow at this tragedy.

When Laertes returns from France after hearing about his father's sudden death he embraces the idea of turning avenger because he sees it as a duty bound up with his sense of 'macho' honour.

He quickly manages to mobilise a group of Danes as hot-headed as himself when he thinks that Claudius may be implicit in the crime. Laertes undertakes to stage a mini-rebellion, all on his own, forcing his way into the palace and confronting Claudius. He certainly shows bravery, initiative and recklessness, all of which contrast dramatically with Hamlet's hesitant, indecisive approach.

Are we intended, however, to admire Laertes for his stance and to condemn Hamlet for his failure to be more like Laertes? Undoubtedly, Laertes's 'giantlike' rebellion was potentially a threat to Claudius: the Danish mob could be heard enthusiastically calling for a coup d'état: 'Choose we; Laertes shall be king!' Of course the threat is quickly dissipated in the face of Claudius's admirable cool-headedness, but again the implicit contrast with Hamlet's failure to do what Laertes had done so effectively is dramatically evident here.

However, when we examine the tone of what Laertes says on the subject of revenge, we can see where the flaws in his approach lie:

> That drop of blood that's calm, proclaims me bastard,
> Cries cuckold to my father, brands the harlot
> Even between the chaste unsmirch'd brows
> Of my true mother
> . . .
> How came he dead? . . .
> To hell, allegiance! Vows to the blackest devil . . .

I dare damnation. To this point I stand
That both the world, I give to negligence,
Let come what comes; only I'll be reveng'd
Most throughly for my father.

Note the quality of the language used throughout here: it is histrionic, strained, over-dramatic and essentially overdone. Laertes is behaving here less out of conviction, less out of genuine grief for his father's death, and more out of a feeling that this is how he should be seen to behave. Later, we will see him behave in the same 'spectacular' fashion at Ophelia's grave. It is not that Laertes is insincere in his attitude to his father's death, but rather that his approach is shallow, superficial, 'showy', too unquestioning and, hence, to some degree suspect. The very fact that he declares himself free of all moral scruples in his desire for revenge, and even more that he 'dares damnation' in the interests of revenge should alert us to the too absolute nature of his approach to the exaction of revenge.

Later, when he has been convinced that Hamlet, not Claudius, killed his father, he adopts the same spectacularly absolutist approach to the prince as the object of his hatred as Claudius had been earlier. When Claudius asks him 'What would you undertake/To show yourself your father's son in deed/More than in words?' Laertes responds in the same provocatively overdone fashion that we have come to expect from him: 'To cut his throat i'the church'.

Despite the superficiality of Laertes's approach to revenge, it may still come as a surprise to an audience to see how easily he succumbs to Claudius's clever manipulation of him into becoming a willing accessory of the king's own plot against Hamlet's life. We should not be altogether surprised, however, as Claudius has already been revealed as a formidable exploiter of the weaknesses of others, and this of course is another aspect of his role in the play as a whole. Indeed, not only does Laertes readily agree to use an 'unbated foil' in the fencing contest that is to take place between himself and Hamlet, he goes a stage further into villainy, beyond what Claudius could have expected of him, by suggesting that he should ensure that Hamlet will not simply be wounded, but killed.

And yet Laertes is no natural villain, and when it comes down to it he feels uneasy at the prospect of what he has planned to do: 'And yet 'tis almost 'gainst my conscience' he admits in an aside. Finally, of course, like Rosencrantz and Guildenstern he finds himself 'hoist with his own petar': 'I am justly killed with mine own treachery', he admits. Before he dies, he seeks to make amends to Hamlet, exposes Claudius's guilt, and asks forgiveness of the men he had wronged. Thus he does not die quite unredeemed, and not quite gracelessly. Hamlet himself is more than ready to forgive him, for already he has expressed his sense of their shared burden: 'by the image of my cause, I see/The portraiture of his.'

Clearly, what was true of Rosencrantz and Guildenstern was also true of Laertes: he has 'come between the pass and fell incensed points/Of mighty opposites', just as they did, and has suffered the consequences.

Laertes dies a victim of his own guile and treachery. Yet his death is different from that of Claudius—we witness Laertes's efforts to repent and ask Hamlet's forgiveness. Laertes is in many ways an important figure in this tragedy as he acts as a foil for Hamlet and also underlines how easy it is to fall victim to corruption and evil-doing.

FORTINBRAS

Fortinbras is the son of Old Fortinbras, the King of Norway, who was defeated by Old Hamlet in battle. Old Fortinbras, like Old Hamlet, is now dead, and his son is trying to regain some lands lost by his father to the Danish king. Young Fortinbras is described in very clear and very vivid terms as a passionate figure, 'Of unimproved mettle/hot and full.'

Like Hamlet, Young Fortinbras is a prince and a leader of men. When we first hear about him, we learn that he has

Shark'd up a list of lawless resolutes
For food and diet, to some enterprise
That hath a stomach in't.

He has mobilised these men to fight against Norway in order to regain the lands that have been lost. In accepting so speedily the principle of avenging his father he resembles Laertes, who also sets about vengeance with a rigorous zeal. Both of these men's characters contrast with Hamlet's inaction and indecisiveness.

We hear very little about Fortinbras once the ambassadors Voltemand and Cornelius have returned successfully from Denmark and managed to convince his uncle to avert his attempts at warring with Denmark. It is only in Act IV, Scene iv, when Fortinbras's army marches across the lands of Denmark on the way to attacking Poland that we hear more about him. In this context, Hamlet has agonised for many hours about trying to revenge himself on Claudius. Hamlet is on the way to England and on seeing the opportunism of young Fortinbras uses this as an excuse to chastise himself again on his delay. But Shakespeare does not just leave this incident on this level. In a deeply condemnatory soliloquy, Hamlet not only chastises himself for lack of action and too much philosophising, but he is also used here as a vehicle to criticise the action of Fortinbras.

We learn that Fortinbras is prepared to sacrifice the lives of twenty thousand men for a mere 'fantasy', a 'trick of fame'—in other words, a piece of land that is not large enough to bury the men. In many ways Shakespeare is asking us to consider the morality of war, and the sacred quality of human life, together with the whole question of honour and nobility.

There can be no doubt about Fortinbras's courage: he will never have to accuse himself of cowardly inaction, as Hamlet has cause to do. Instead, in Hamlet's words about him, Fortinbras

> Makes mouths at the invisible event
> Exposing what is mortal and unsure
> To all that fortune, death and danger dare
> Even for an eggshell.

Fortinbras therefore can be seen as courageous, spirited and enterprising, a model military leader or warrior hero. At the conclusion of the play the crown of Denmark becomes his for the taking. With the cool opportunism we have already seen in him he takes what is on offer, makes all the right gestures, says and does what is appropriate, dignified and magnanimous: the future is his. We do not have to pick our brains as to the kind of king he will make: like the elder Hamlet, he will be a warrior monarch. The wheel appears to have come full circle.

ROSENCRANTZ AND GUILDENSTERN

These are two former school friends of Hamlet who are employed by Claudius in order to 'glean' what underlines his unusual behaviour or 'antic disposition'. The two men operate almost as one character: each has little identity apart from the other. In their language and behaviour in the play they simply echo one another or simply confirm what the other has said.

In the case of these two characters, *role* dominates over character. In other words, their function in the play is to highlight how powerful Claudius is, and the lengths he will go to in order to suppress his nephew from finding out the truth about Old Hamlet. The fact that they were friends of Hamlet and yet they are prepared to spy on him and betray his friendship is another indication of how deeply 'rotten' the state of Denmark has become under Claudius's rule.

From the outset, when Hamlet greets them and they begin to engage in dubious sentiments about honesty and ambition, there is a distinct note of suspicion in his reactions to his two friends. Shortly after meeting with them he manages to force them to acknowledge, however begrudgingly, that 'we were sent for'. Hamlet knows now the reasons why they have been summoned to Elsinore, and from now on he will treat them with a certain degree of contempt and derision. He knows they are mere pawns of the king and so in his dealings with them he will use his 'antic disposition' at will.

When, after staging 'The Mousetrap', Hamlet manages to prove the Ghost's story true, he is not slow to attack them for trying to 'play upon me' and 'pluck out the heart of my mystery'. The images Hamlet uses to expose the reality of these two men is very fitting. He calls them sponges 'that soaks up the king's countenance, his rewards, and his authorities'.

Rosencrantz and Guildenstern, who made 'love to this employment', who were complicit in trying to organise the death of Hamlet, die as victims of their own evil-doing—just like Claudius and Laertes. Hamlet, having discovered the plot to take his life, manages to change the details of the letter to the King of England and Rosencrantz and Guildenstern are put to death instead.

These two men come between two mighty forces—Hamlet and Claudius—and meet their death:

> 'Tis dangerous when the baser nature comes
> Between the pass and fell incensed points
> Of mighty opposites.

Both these characters serve to highlight once more the power of Claudius's hold on the kingdom and at the same time the range and scope of the corruption seeping through the kingdom. Like all the evil characters in this play, they end up as victims of their own corrupt plotting—further evidence of the self-destructive quality of evil-doing.

THEMES

FALSE APPEARANCE AND REALITY

At every stage in this play the issue of false appearance and reality is mentioned in some way. Everything in the play in enmeshed in the web of 'seeming'. All through the play the characters and the audience are disturbed by the problematic nature of reality and appearance. The very mechanism that sets the action going, the Ghost of Hamlet's father, is, in the eyes of those who encounter it, of dubious origin and significance. He may be, to use Hamlet's words, 'a spirit of health or goblin damn'd'; he may be, Horatio thinks, some fiend sent to lure Hamlet to his ruin. And yet this phantom heralds some painful realities for Hamlet and the court of Claudius.

The opening of the play sets the atmosphere with the references to the appearance of a ghostly figure at night. Opening with a series of terse, nervous insinuations about the supernatural, the play throws us immediately into another world where we are not sure what is true and what is false. From the outset, in the equivocal and nervous language of Marcellus and Barnardo, we as audience find that we are facing a world where darkness, uncertainty, equivocation and ambiguity dominate. We hear about the ghost as a strange thing, that its presence spells out the idea that 'something is rotten in the state of Denmark'.

The world of Elsinore is a world of 'things hidden'. We realise very soon that many people here live a life of hypocrisy, they play false roles. Claudius makes an impressive appearance in Act I, Scene ii, just after he has received the crown of Denmark in the immediate aftermath of his brother's sudden death. Initially, Claudius appears to be an excellent monarch who expresses due concern and understanding about people's grief over his brother's death, and who manages to avert the attack from Fortinbras with a skilful political expertise. Claudius manages people very skilfully: the supreme diplomat, he deftly handles all manner of conflict and difficulty with a speedy diligence. And so we as audience are impressed with this able monarch who is in control and who manifests an almost paternal concern for the welfare and security of his country and those within it.

Gertrude as queen also represents the embodiment of the perfect monarch's wife as she dutifully continues her role as queen with another man. Her quiet, tactful loyalty to her new husband Claudius and her ready obedience to all his commands are almost worthy of praise.

But these impressions are soon dispelled with the Ghost's revelations to Hamlet a few days later. With the Ghost's words about the manner of his death and the true nature of Claudius and Gertrude ('adulterate beast' and 'seeming virtuous queen') we realise that the play is operating on many different levels. It is these different levels—what *appears to be* the case, and what actually *is* the case—that contribute to the predominance of the issue of false appearance and reality that governs the entire plot.

As events unfold, and as reality emerges from behind the façade of falsity and glittering appearance, we discover a different version of Claudius. We learn that he is a 'smiling damned villain' while Gertrude is a queen who is 'seeming virtuous', but is in fact a faithless adulteress. We become aware of the 'seeming' at the heart of being in Claudius's self-enclosed little court world. 'These are actions that a man might play,' Hamlet tells his mother. Everyone at Elsinore is playing a false part, all are hypocrites, from Claudius down to the most obscure courtier Osric.

We learn how Rosencrantz and Guildenstern, who come to the palace under the guise of being old school friends of Hamlet, are in fact working as spies for the king. The king's counsellor of state Polonius seems to be a wise and good old man making harmless small talk with Hamlet, yet in reality he is a devious politician trying to 'draw him out' and manipulate him for corrupt reasons. When Ophelia appears in the corridor she appears to be an innocent young girl reading from a pious book, whereas in reality she is being used as puppet by her father in order to trap Hamlet and uncover what is going on in his mind.

As a result of the Ghost's revelations about Denmark's 'disjointed' time and of the rottenness at its core, all gestures of friendship, all courtly attendance and all joking commentary, the apparently innocent comings and goings between people, take on a much darker and much more dubious colouring.

It is interesting that when Hamlet hears about Claudius's deed of murder from the Ghost he decides to adopt an 'antic disposition' or a strategy whereby he will deal with the news and try to uncover the truth that underlies the lies and falsity endemic in the court of Elsinore. This 'antic disposition', or cloak of madness, takes several forms. Hamlet uses language to confuse and disorient people, but this is part of his strategy to try to get to the truth underlying things.

Hamlet also uses gestures and ambiguous forms of action and speech designed to help him find the truth. These gestures, and Hamlet's use of language, become more hysterical as the play develops. Hamlet begins to doubt even the nature and authenticity of the Ghost as time unfolds: he wonders whether it may be a 'goblin damn'd' or a true figure of his father, and he will confirm this by staging a play. After having caught the conscience of the reigning monarch, Hamlet finds him praying in his chapel and decides that he cannot kill him now because he will go straight to heaven. This is another instance of the theme of false appearance and reality. Here the king appears a saintly figure close to redemption and to his creator. The reality, however, his inner disposition, which is hidden from Hamlet, is different:

> My words fly up, my thoughts remain below
> Words without thoughts never to heaven go.

And in fact Claudius fails to repent of his deeds at any time in the play.

In the Closet Scene it would appear that there are only two people present—Hamlet and his mother—but Polonius is hiding behind the arras with the intention of listening to the conversation between Hamlet and his mother and reporting it to the king. When Hamlet is invited to engage in a fencing duel with Laertes it would appear to be a piece of entertainment on the part of the king, while the reality is that one of the swords has been treated with poison in order to kill Hamlet efficiently. Certainly, throughout this play Shakespeare appears intent on showing us that appearances are not all they seem, that there is another reality underneath, which must be exposed.

This theme of reality and appearance finds expression in the play in a profoundly rich pattern of imagery and language. Images of paintings, cloaking and acting dominate in the play, vividly highlighting the impression of insincerity and falsity.

Even Hamlet himself falls victim to this cloaking of reality in his assumption of the 'antic disposition', which is a mask enabling him to hide and conceal his motivations. Indeed, it could be said that Hamlet himself remains an enigma right to the end: we are unable to 'pluck out the heart of his mystery' or ever be sure what lies at the root of his mindset and behaviour.

Hamlet's gentle invocation to Horatio to remain alive and refrain from drinking from the poisoned chalice would seem to indicate that truth finally wins out in the end. Even though the dead bodies that strew the stage at the conclusion betoken a battlefield more than a gracious palace, Horatio will remain strong and steadfast in this desire to vindicate the truth of the lives of those who lie dead.

It can be said that to a certain degree reality and truth do triumph in the end, with the destruction of what is evil and with a certain restoration of order and harmony within the political and social framework of Denmark.

POWER AND KINGSHIP

From the beginning of the play we hear about the type of power and kingship exercised by Hamlet's father, Old Hamlet. It seems he was a natural leader of men, a man of action who was cast in the heroic mould. Horatio remembers him fondly when he was fighting the 'sledded Polacks on the ice'. Hamlet, his son, has even fonder memories of Old Hamlet and the type of leadership he wielded as king—he describes him in terms of a demi-god, a Hyperion, the font of Jove with 'an eye like Mars'. For Hamlet he represented the ideal king, noble, awe-inspiring and unmistakably royal, who fought on behalf of his country as a warrior king. It is interesting that when he appears on stage as the Ghost he is still clad in the military armour that he would have worn during his lifetime, and is thus more easily recognised by the soldiers and by Horatio. When he makes his appearance on the night the guards are watching over Elsinore it is striking that all men connect his appearance with a direct threat to Denmark itself, and they use strong words: 'something is rotten in the state of Denmark.'

Certainly the pictures given to us of Old Hamlet suggest that he was an ideal and idealised leader of men, a monarch who inspired true respect in his subjects, and who risked his life in the service of his country.

In contrast, at the start of the play, the country of Denmark has a new king, a usurper king who in some ways could be described as the antithesis or dramatic opposite of his brother Old Hamlet. When viewed in a superficial light, Claudius appears an efficient and capable ruler, a skilful diplomat quick to avert all threats to his own security and that of his kingdom. He is different from his brother in that he achieves his ends by means of rhetoric and the smooth manipulation of people, rather than through actual warfare.

Likewise, his tactics are based more on opportunism and political manoeuvring than by operating with a sense of integrity or heroism. It would seem that Claudius's foreign policy is more defensive than offensive. In relation to Fortinbras he will defend the country against attack, but he also, and more characteristically, sends a diplomatic mission to the king of Norway, Fortinbras's uncle, demanding that the latter restrain his bellicose nephew. Claudius's strategies are always designed to remove obstacles as quickly as possible, to give the impression of a ruler who gets things done without any delay. Claudius is effective in this respect. Hamlet comments bitterly how the Danes are prepared to pay large sums of money in order to acquire his 'portrait in little'. Earlier, the Ghost had commented with equal bitterness on the 'witchcraft of his wit' in seducing Gertrude, and Hamlet sums up what he sees as the most offensive quality in his uncle: 'That one may smile, and smile, and be a villain.' He is a smooth-talking, superficial man who consistently hides behind a smiling exterior.

As king and leader, Claudius is Machiavellian in the most devious sense. His intention at every stage is to 'bear all smooth and even', and to appear to consult his chief courtiers at every stage. He is constantly worried about public opinion and how it will affect his reign as monarch, and therefore he needs to find a plausible excuse to dispatch Hamlet to England: 'This sudden sending him away must seem/Deliberate pause.'

However, Claudius is no coward. We witness this fact repeatedly. He shows a masterful calm and enormous power in confronting and dealing with Laertes's 'giantlike rebellion'. Claudius is a formidable manipulator. He concocts a cunning and devious scheme with Laertes so that in the aftermath of Hamlet's planned death:

> … no wind shall breathe
> But even his mother shall uncharge the practice
> And call it accident.

It is no wonder therefore that Hamlet sees Claudius as a 'vice of kings', and finally comes to view himself as bound by patriotic and moral duty to put an end to the life of this 'canker of our nature' before it brings 'further evil'.

It is Claudius's lust for power that sustains all his actions and contriving in the play. He tells us that he killed his brother for the sake of 'My crown, mine own ambition, and my queen.' Claudius is also avid for the pleasures of life, and his court reflects his own self-indulgent sensuality. Elsinore under Claudius will therefore not be the Elsinore of his predecessor. Claudius loves the 'swagg'ring upspring reels', enjoys lengthy bouts of carousing, and seems to be very much at home with the pleasure-loving courtiers. He even looks with a certain degree of indulgence at the young Laertes, who wishes to return to the centre of pleasure, Paris, and sow his wild oats: 'Take thy fair hour, Laertes.'

Claudius's rule, then, like his exercise of power, is corrupt and flawed in its essence since it is based on murder, incest and usurpation of a power that is not his by right. The smooth, smiling exterior never quite conceals the formidable ruthlessness that is central to his nature. Above all else, Claudius is a survivor. At the very end, we find him clinging tenaciously to power as he does to life even while both are ebbing relentlessly away from him: 'O, yet defend me, friends! I am but hurt.'

Radically different types of kingship and methods of exercising power are shown to us through these two men, Claudius and Old Hamlet. It is certainly clear that Old Hamlet's Elsinore would not have encouraged Danish drinking habits, and that the worldly amorality and materialism that was a hallmark of Claudius's court was not the spirit of the court presided over by Old Hamlet.

VENGEANCE AND FILIAL DUTY

Filial duty is a major theme in *Hamlet*. It is examined not only in the main plot but also in the subplot. It is also closely linked to the theme of revenge that is central to the play.

Three men lose their fathers either before or during the play—Hamlet, Laertes and Fortinbras. Hamlet's father has been murdered by Claudius, the reigning King of Denmark. Laertes's father Polonius is killed by Hamlet while he is spying on him behind the arras. Fortinbras, a young prince of Norway, lost his father when he was killed in battle by Old Hamlet.

Revenge is a traditional theme in drama, going back to Greek and Roman tragedies. In this play Shakespeare examines the different approaches to filial revenge. However, here the theme is complicated by the Christian concepts of justice and retribution (especially in the case of Hamlet).

The revenge of Fortinbras is **political**. He has 'Shark'd up a list of lawless resolutes/For food and diet . . .' in order to '. . . recover of us, by strong hand . . . those foresaid lands . . .' This enterprise is nipped in the bud when Claudius dispatches Cornelius and Voltemand to 'Old Norway' to put a stop to the activities of Fortinbras—'to suppress/His further gait herein . . .' This is a splendid political move, contributing to Claudius's political image even more.

Fortinbras's dispute is resolved purely within the law. He '...makes vow before his uncle never more/To give th'assay of arms against your majesty ...'

It is ironic that at the end of the play, Fortinbras gains not only the disputed territory but all the kingdom of Denmark as well. 'For me, with sorrow, I embrace my fortune.' It should be noted that, unlike Hamlet's, the revenge of Fortinbras involves no philosophising, no wondering if the right cause is being pursued. It is based purely on a political decision.

Young Laertes has one of the strongest motives for revenge in the play. When he returns from France he finds, tragically, he has 'a noble father lost;/A sister driven into desp'rate terms'. Laertes, in his frenzy of grief and eagerness for revenge, rushes into a corrupt deal with Claudius. Laertes seems to accept the ethic of revenge almost as a duty to a father who has been killed. Revenge is related to a sense of honour for Laertes, and so he embraces it quickly, unlike Hamlet, who spends a great deal of time in agonising. Laertes's stance here is quite histrionic and dramatic, and he uses flamboyant language:

> That drop of blood that's calm proclaims me bastard;
> Cries cuckold to my father; brands the harlot
> Even here between the chaste unsmirched brows
> Of my true mother.
>
> . . .

How came he dead? I'll not be juggled with:
To hell, allegiance! vows, to the blackest devil

…

I dare damnation. To this point I stand,
That both the worlds, I give to negligence,
Let come what comes; only I'll be reveng'd
Most throughly for my father.

It is not that Laertes is insincere in his attitude to his father's death, but rather that his approach is shallow, superficial, 'showy', too unquestioning, and therefore to some degree suspect. The very fact that he declares himself free of all moral scruples in his desire for revenge and, even more, that he 'dares damnation' in the interests of vengeance, should alert us to the too absolute nature of his approach to the exaction of revenge.

Later, when he has been convinced that Hamlet, not Claudius, killed his father, he adopts the same spectacularly absolutist approach to the prince as object of his hatred as Claudius had been earlier. When Claudius asks him, 'What would'st thou undertake/To show thyself thy father's son in deed more than words?', Laertes responds in the same provocatively overdone fashion that we have come to expect from him: 'To cut his throat i'the church'. Laertes's anger has destroyed his sense of morality. Laertes, however, is not a natural villain. He feels uneasy about the corrupt plot engineered by Claudius. When Hamlet injures him with the poisoned sword, Laertes realises his own wickedness:

Why, as a woodcock to mine own springe …
I am justly killed with mine own treachery.

Before he dies Laertes seeks to make amends to Hamlet by asking him forgiveness. Hamlet is quick to forgive Laertes, knowing as he does that both men have become in some way victims of a larger plot that originated with Claudius.

Hamlet and revenge

Hamlet also has strong motives for revenge: his father has been murdered and his mother seduced by the murderer, Claudius. Hamlet has been denied the right to succeed his father. His need and resolve to avenge his father is strengthened immeasurably by the appearance of the ghost of his dead father, who instantly orders Hamlet to take revenge: 'Revenge his foul and most unnatural murder.' Despite these powerful injunctions to carry out revenge, and despite the undoubted justification in terms of filial duty, Hamlet remains throughout the entire play in the position of reluctant avenger:

> … O cursed spite
> That ever I was born to set it right!

Hamlet differs from both Fortinbras and Laertes in that he refuses to rush into vengeance but instead examines the question and its consequences very carefully. He debates within himself about the issue of the Ghost, considering that he may be a devil who 'abuses me to damn me'.

In many respects, the Ghost's command is a futile act. Neither the Ghost himself nor obedience to his command can restore the lost innocence of his mother or relieve Hamlet's sense of shock and betrayal. Nor can vengeance restore Old Hamlet to the throne of Denmark. However, none of these points is acknowledged by Hamlet. From the time when Hamlet meets the Ghost his behaviour begins to disintegrate. There is a distinct impression that Hamlet's conscience is in revolt against his task of revenge, and that this task violates his deepest instincts. In this respect, Hamlet's delay in carrying out the command to avenge his father is quite justifiable. Moreover, Hamlet has deep misgivings about the validity of the Ghost. This is not given full expression until after the Players arrive. Here, in the Hecuba soliloquy, he expresses for the first time in the play his concern that, 'The spirit that I have seen/May be a devil.'

'The Mousetrap' is a very effective act of vengeance against Claudius. Shortly after the success of 'The Mousetrap', Hamlet encounters Claudius while he is praying in his private chapel and again refrains from acting, seeking another excuse to delay:

> A villain kills my father; and for that
> I, his sole son, do this same villain send
> To heaven.

He decides that his revenge must be absolute. It must involve not only the death of Claudius's body but the destruction of his soul as well. Killing Claudius at prayer is '… hire and salary …' No! He must be killed

> … when he is drunk asleep; or in his rage;
> Or in th' incestuous pleasure of his bed . . .

Hamlet wants his revenge to be as potent as Claudius's murder. There seems to be a deep incompatibility between Hamlet's behaviour as an avenger here and the Christian sentiments that are a constant feature of his character throughout the play.

Hamlet's attack on his mother following this scene could constitute another stage in his revenge. He announces his intention as he sets off to visit her chamber:

> Let me be cruel, not unnatural;
> I will speak daggers to her, but use none.

In the Closet Scene, Hamlet's vengeance is directed at his mother. Here, in a violent tirade, he attacks his mother and forces her to face up to her guilt and her behaviour. Hamlet does succeed in evoking the correct response from the queen, as her words confirm:

> O Hamlet, speak no more!
> Thou turn'st mine eyes into my very soul,
> And there I see such black and grained spots
> As will not leave their tinct.

Hamlet's speedy departure to England after this scene prevents him from immediately fulfilling his intention to murder Claudius while he is in an act of damnation. On Hamlet's return to Denmark in Act V, Scene i, there is a distinct change in his whole attitude to revenge. Hamlet's mood now is more serene and optimistic. His attitude is that of a Christian prince who knows that things will work out. Hamlet no longer consciously schemes, instead he calmly reasons that, 'There's a divinity that shapes our ends.'

He sees his role as avenger in a new light, he no longer chastises himself with his delay but sees himself almost as an agent of divine justice: 'Why even in this was heaven ordinant . . . there's a special providence in the fall of a sparrow.'

His death is peaceful and his attitude in death is one of equanimity. This sense of peace stems from an attitude that he is animated by the guiding or benevolent hand of providence.

It is quite clear that Shakespeare does not want us to see his hero as the man of action that Fortinbras and Laertes seem to be. Neither of them hesitates to carry out what they see as their duty to exact revenge. Both Laertes and Fortinbras accommodate quite easily and happily to their roles as avengers, and proceed to 'sweep to their revenge', and they both see their personal honour at stake if they fail to carry out what they see as their clear filial duty. In Hamlet's case the issue is much more complex.

At the conclusion of the play Hamlet has acquired a new serenity and self-command.

He has now fully accepted that to fail to kill Claudius, 'this canker of our nature', is to ensure his own damnation, and equally, he is now convinced he is in the hands of God and that Heaven will provide him with the right circumstances and the right opportunity to carry out this essential act.

So resigned is he to his fate that when Horatio offers a tentative warning about Hamlet committing himself to the fencing match with Laertes, the prince dismisses the warning, declaring that he is ready for whatever awaits him:

> If it be now, 'tis not to come …
> the readiness is all.

He can now accept the prospect of imminent death with tranquil equanimity: 'Since no man owes aught of what he leaves, what is't to leave betimes?'

Hamlet, then, has finally accommodated himself to the role of avenger, but only to the extent that he now sees himself as the passive instrument of destiny: 'Even in that was Heaven ordinant'; 'There is a special providence in the fall of a sparrow'; 'The interim is mine/And a man's life is no more than to say "one".' We sense the decisive purpose behind his quiet words: 'I am constant to my purposes; they follow the king's pleasure', and so we are prepared for that final flurry of action where Hamlet disposes of Claudius with lethal, unhesitating efficiency.

Throughout the entire play Hamlet has been involved in a private 'war' in which he has been fighting against evil. He may have become hardened and even brutalised in the course of this prolonged and secret conflict, yet he is ultimately on the side of the angels. Therefore we, as audience, are expected to accept the propriety of Horatio's final tribute to Hamlet:

> Good-night, sweet prince;
> And flights of angels sing thee to thy rest.

The lesson of the play from the perspective of revenge is that it is always destructive and engulfs the innocent as well as the guilty. Perhaps it is Shakespeare's wish to show that the need for vengeance, however strong the motive, costs too much.

THE MOTHER FIGURE

The two main female characters in *Hamlet* are Gertrude, the reigning queen of Denmark, and Ophelia, the young daughter of the chief counsellor of state, Polonius. In the predominantly male world of Elsinore, neither of these two women is strong or dominant: in fact, they both become passive instruments or pawns in the hands of male manipulators.

From the opening scenes of the play Gertrude seems to occupy an inordinately excessive amount of time in young Hamlet's mind and preoccupations. One could say that it is truly ironic that such a morally sensitive young man as Hamlet could happen to have a woman such as Gertrude for his mother. Gertrude is still a beautiful woman who is well aware of her attractiveness: maybe a character such as this is more appropriate to a bedroom comedy than a tragic play. She is too merry a widow, and we realise very soon in the play how lust can still 'mutine in a matron's bones'. She is evidently the type of woman who cannot do without a man. Hamlet's attitude to his parents' marriage is similar to an idealistic adolescent who sees both people and their marriage as a remote, unassailable perfection. Tragically, however, it would seem that even in her husband's lifetime Gertrude succumbed to sensual weakness and the 'witchcraft' of Claudius, so that her 'seeming' virtue is a sham. As queen she probably became an adulteress before she entered into an incestuous marriage with her husband's brother.

It is because of this behaviour on the part of his mother that Hamlet's vision of the world has become irrevocably darkened, and that he sees all women from now on as potential betrayers. It also accounts for his hostile and violent attitude towards Ophelia. Women are frail, the world has become an 'unweeded garden', while he sees his own flesh as sullied because of Gertrude's sin.

In the first encounter in the play between mother and son, Shakespeare seems to be intent on highlighting the fact that Gertrude is a woman who is completely blind to the reality of her situation. She seconds Claudius's attempts to rally Hamlet from his melancholy mood and to help him come to terms with his father's death:

> Thou knows 'tis common. All that lives must die,
> Passing through nature to eternity.

While there is a certain degree of common sense here, it is also evident from the way Hamlet reacts that she fails to empathise at all with her son. His vehement riposte demonstrates to the audience that Hamlet is fostering deep within him some strong condemnations of his mother's behaviour:

> Like Niobe, all tears …
> O, most wicked speed, to post
> With such dexterity to incestuous sheets!

Gertrude does love her son, and is concerned and uneasy about his state of mind. She is shrewd enough to sense that his mindset has something to do with 'our o'erhasty marriage'. Yet Gertrude has no problem fitting very naturally into the world of 'seeming' created by Claudius. Gertrude is totally at home in the brilliant and materialistic microcosm of Elsinore, with its frenetic lust for life, its emphasis on the here and now, its debased value systems and its acceptance of the status quo. Her brief mourning for her dead husband was a matter merely of assuming the 'trappings and the suits of woe'. From the very outset of the play, she is part of the rottenness at the heart of Denmark. She can pose decorously as the 'Imperial jointress of the State', taken to wife by the newly elected King of Denmark, Claudius, for reasons of state, but the truth about her position is uglier. She is silly, superficial and amoral, and like her new husband animated constantly by a desire to 'bear all smooth and even'.

Gertrude is as eager as Claudius to have Rosencrantz and Guildenstern, Hamlet's old school friends, 'draw ... on to pleasures' her 'too much changed son'. However, Gertrude has to face the fact that her son continues to be a brooding, depressed presence who poses an increasing danger in the court, and is a constant tacit reminder to her of her failure as mother and wife. Worse still, he seems to have been driven dangerously mad as a result of her own behaviour. A good deal of Gertrude's tragedy lies in her moral myopia: in her 'not noticing and not understanding', in the words of one critic.

Gertrude's vision is limited and confined to the material world. She cannot understand anything other than the events of this world. Thus, in the Closet Scene, when the ghost of her dead husband appears before her, Gertrude cannot see the spirit. She sees 'Nothing at all; yet all that is I see'. She sees the material world, 'all that is', and nothing beyond it. The tragedy in this brief domestic interlude lies in the irrevocable severing of husband and son from the woman whose attenuated moral vision has led her to betray both of them.

It is not until this particular episode—the Closet Scene, Act III, Scene iv, following the play within a play—that Gertrude comes to an understanding of what her position has been. Her unfeigned horror at Hamlet's accusation, 'A bloody deed—almost as bad, good mother,/As kill a king and marry with his brother', makes clear her innocence and lack of complicity in the murder of her first husband. As the interview proceeds, however, Gertrude begins to see herself with new and horrified eyes. Initially Hamlet's wild words and manner begin to alarm her: 'Thou wilt not murther me?' she cries in terror, when he flings her back into a chair and talks about setting her up 'a glass where you may see the inmost part of you'. Mindful of Polonius behind the arras, she calls for help, only to have the eavesdropper killed in her presence. Subdued and terrified, but still uncomprehending, the mother is now forced to sit and listen to her son lecture her on her moral shortcomings. Gertrude is so thoroughly a part of Claudius's world that at first she can make out little of what her son says. What does he mean by his wild talk of an 'act that blurs the grace and blush of modesty;/Calls virtue hypocrite', turns 'sweet religion' into 'a rhapsody of words'? His intellectualised generalisations mean nothing to his shallow-minded mother, so he uses a method not unlike the play within the play earlier, by producing two pictures—the 'counterfeit presentment' of the dead king and his living brother—and, by contrasting one with the other, seeks to show his mother the truth behind her own preference for Claudius, the pseudo king and satyr, over Hamlet, the real king and godlike man.

She has taken appearance for reality, has left the 'fair mountain' to 'batten on this moor'. What she calls love is basest lust, and of all her faculties Hamlet lays most blame on her reason, which has acted as 'pander' to her will. As Hamlet describes Gertrude's relationship with Claudius in ever grosser images, he finally wears her down, so that she comes to see herself through his outraged eyes.

> O Hamlet, speak no more!
> Thou turn'st mine eyes into my very soul,
> And there I see such black and grained spots
> As will not leave their tinct.

Gertrude has now become awakened to the nature of her own guilt and more aware of her husband Claudius's real character. She listens humbly to her son and begins to ask with a bewildered sense of uncertainty, 'What shall I do?', as she promises Hamlet not to reveal what has occurred between them.

After this long and rather harrowing interview with her son, Gertrude moves into the shadows, now no longer a focal point in the drama. She appears with Claudius in the subsequent court scenes, but says little and seems removed from much of the action about her. She seeks to disarm criticism of Hamlet by excusing him in terms of his madness, and she appears to have withdrawn herself from Claudius, though this is merely hinted at here and there. In a significant aside in Act IV, Scene v she refers to her 'sick soul' and to sin's 'true nature', suggesting a deep and settled depressive condition. In her sensitive and moving account of Ophelia's death and her sad comment as she later strews flowers over the grave, there is perhaps further evidence that Hamlet's admonitions have had their effect on her better nature.

She dies with a dire poetic justice, as a result of her husband's failure to save her. Claudius, in his fashion, loves Gertrude, his 'mouse' as he calls her, but his own instinct for survival is stronger than his feelings for his wife. When he sees her lift the poisoned cup to her lips, he moves instinctively to prevent her from drinking its contents, and then, aware that he would betray himself if he intervened, holds back in guilty silence. Gertrude's death goes almost unnoticed by the audience; all eyes are focused on the final clash of those 'mighty opposites', Hamlet and Claudius. Her epitaph is a mere cursory afterthought on Hamlet's part: 'Wretched queen, adieu.'

Gertrude's role is important in the play in many ways. In her moral obtuseness, she is an integral aspect of the moral topsy-turvy value system operative in that world, a world where sons must lecture mothers and remind them that 'when you are desirous to be blest,/I'll blessing beg of you'. Finally of course, and above all, Gertrude is Hamlet's mother and our chief interest in her derives from our interest in him.

DEATH

The brooding presence of death is oppressively manifest throughout this play. We as audience are never allowed to stray far from the consideration of human mortality, within the confines of the play's action, since imagery and incident alike keep this theme insistently, even obsessively, present to us. Theatrical reminders of death—Hamlet's mourning clothes, the skull and bones of the graveyard episode—give way to the more graphic miming of violent death in the play within a play, and this in turn to the staged 'reality' of the violent ends of all the play's protagonists.

Death in this play has about it little of the tragic grandeur and dignity with which it is associated in Shakespeare's other tragedies: the deaths that occur in this drama are messy affairs, ugly, untidy hurryings into eternity. Polonius is unceremoniously killed like a rat, while spying behind the arras; his body is buried 'hugger mugger', having been first gruesomely lugged about, and then hidden under a stairway, by his murderer. Ugly reality breaks in even on the lyrical narrative of the queen's account of Ophelia's death: the 'poor wretch' is pulled to 'muddy death'.

Hamlet's father died horribly by the poison administered to him by Claudius, his body covered in a 'lazar-like' encrustation, 'bark'd about' with 'vile and loathsome crust'. Rosencrantz and Guildenstern are executed on arrival in England, 'no shriving time allowed'. Laertes dies ignobly on his own poisoned sword, his 'foul practice' turning upon himself. The unfortunate Gertrude dies by the poison prepared by her husband for her son, and as a result of her husband's failure to save her life by means of a timely warning. Claudius is 'doubly' slain by Hamlet—first with a thrust of the poisoned rapier, then by being forced to drink to the dregs the poisoned potion he had himself prepared for Hamlet. Hamlet himself is dying even as he kills his enemy. Death is at the heart of all the staged events in this play.

The revenge theme itself, which is the mainspring of the plot, is inevitably death-centred: in this play, hunter and hunted alike seek the life of the other, in a murderous game of 'cat and mouse', involving the casual slaughter of those only peripherally involved in the central intrigue.

The play is set in motion by a figure from beyond the grave, the spirit of the man lately dead, who had in his lifetime ruled as absolute monarch in Denmark, but who is now a 'thing', making the 'night hideous' for the living.

The encounters with the Ghost take place at night, in a setting which tempts men to throw themselves to destruction. Hamlet's encounter with the Ghost launches him on a murderous course which will eventually lead to his own death.

The imagery and diction of the play are saturated with insistent reminders of life's frailty and of death's omnipresence. Imagery of poison, corruption, disease and transience are to be found everywhere: 'Rank corruption, mining all within,/Infects unseen'; 'The canker galls the infants of the spring'; 'The fat weed/. . . rots itself in ease on Lethe wharf' . . .

The play's most obviously dominant image patterns are those suggestive of a poisonous corruption, spreading inexorably throughout an organism, with fatal results. Imagery is thus linked with the events of the drama and with the play's moral preoccupations. The play's action merely echoes the message of the imagery. As Hamlet's father died from poisoning, so the chief characters in the play will all themselves be poisoned. Evil centres on Claudius, the original poisoner. From this 'canker of our nature' the corruption spreads outwards, attacking and overthrowing the good, the bad and the merely indifferent alike. Imagery and action are faithful mirror images of one another.

The Graveyard Scene in Act V is a truly powerful and moving comment on death and life. This scene takes place just after the death of Polonius, and after we have heard the conversation between Claudius and Laertes in which they plot to kill Hamlet. This episode thus becomes a poignant and disturbing reminder of the play's obsession with mortality. Yet the treatment of death here is neither particularly morbid nor unwholesome. In the midst of death, the gravediggers remind us, we are 'in life'—and they are very much alive. Their conversations revolve around the fact that death is a great leveller—death, after all, as they themselves have witnessed, brings all men, king and commoner alike, to the same humbling and ultimately anonymous level. Behind the jokes of the gravedigger who sings at his work, however, there is a tragic reminder of death's finality: the houses built by the gravemaker last until doomsday.

At this point Hamlet appears and begins to meditate upon mortality and upon 'the base uses to which we may return', because of the gravedigger's unearthing of skulls. The inevitability of death is clearly evident when we hear the gravedigger answer Hamlet's question about how long he has been working at his trade: 'that very day that young Hamlet was born'. Shakespeare seems to be reminding us that 'in the midst of life we are in death'.

Even before the Ghost's revelation, Hamlet in his first soliloquy is plainly sickened by life and longing for death, restrained in fact from suicide only by his religious scruples. His vision of the world is that of an 'unweeded garden', he is in revolt against the 'too sullied' flesh which holds him bound to an earthly reality that he has come to abhor. This emphasis on death as a desirable end is reinforced when Hamlet learns the full truth of the manner of his father's death. Now he has a positive reinforcement for his hatred of life. Human life he sees now as essentially evil and ugly. Man, that 'paragon of animals' is, after all, but a 'quintessence of dust', and Polonius can do him no greater favour than to relieve him of his life.

In the great 'To be, or not to be' soliloquy Hamlet dallies longingly with the thought of death as a release, but his attitude here is more complex than it was earlier. Life is here seen as a grunting, sweating endurance test, and man can be faced with no greater tragedy than the prospect of living to be old. In contrast, the exhausted mind sees death in the most alluring terms, as a 'quietus', a sleep, a state of non-being, where neither action nor decision are operative or necessary.

Critics have frequently remarked, when discussing Hamlet's preoccupation with death, that it is not death itself that Hamlet truly dreads, but rather the state of being dead. Hamlet is at once revolted and fascinated by the disgusting realities of physical death. Here again, he reveals himself to be a typical Renaissance man, for the Renaissance mind found itself always sensitively and precariously balanced between acute apprehension of and delight in the beauty of the sensory world, and a tragic awareness of mutability.

Again and again, Hamlet forces himself and the audience to confront the repulsive bodily aspects of death:

If the sun breed maggots in a dead dog

...

I'll lug the guts into the neighbour room

...

A certain convocation of politic worms are e'en at him.

Hamlet's problem is that he has not simply suffered the death of a beloved father, he has also had to endure what was for him a greater blow—the outrage of his mother's remarriage. Thus, while his father is irrevocably dead, Gertrude and Claudius are insistently, obtrusively and obscenely alive. Hamlet's life hatred, and his complementary longing for death, centres on his horror at the unnatural union between his uncle and his mother.

When we meet Hamlet in Act V we realise he has come to terms not only with the thought of death, but also with his role as avenger. Instead, he seems to see himself as a passive instrument in the hands of providence, the obedient power which will decide the moment not only of Claudius's demise, but also of his own. Hamlet seems prepared to face his own personal 'moment of truth' with a strangely calm detachment:

> ... we defy augury. There's a special providence in the fall of a sparrow.

The fencing match with Laertes is a theatrical re-enactment of the dangerous cat and mouse game that Hamlet has for so long been playing with Claudius. This, too, despite its element of ritual and ceremonial, is a duel to the death. The disruption of the elaborate trial of gentlemanly skills is followed by a flurry of ever more violent action which leaves the stage littered with corpses: the play's protagonists are either dead or dying before our eyes, and the reality of death has intruded into the world of make-believe.

Fortinbras and Horatio try to make some sort of order and sense out of the chaos and carnage all about them. Hamlet's death comes almost as an anti-climax. He dies quietly and without great drama. Paradoxically, he concentrates in giving his 'dying voice' to ensure the succession of young Fortinbras, while he begs Horatio to 'absent thee from felicity awhile', in order to stay alive and bear witness to the truth of what has happened.

These are the final commentaries on death that linger in our minds when the drama closes, together with Horatio's moving and fitting words of farewell:

> Good-night, sweet prince;
> And flights of angels sing thee to thy rest.

LANGUAGE AND IMAGERY

Imagery plays three important roles in *Hamlet*.

- It creates the atmosphere of tragedy.
- It illustrates certain themes, e.g. deception, corruption, good and evil.
- It helps to reveal the nature of the characters in the play.

There is a distinct emphasis on poisoning in the play. When taken in conjunction with the recurring images of disease and corruption, the emphasis on poisoning assumes a deeper significance: action and imagery echo and reinforce on another, and a unifying pattern clearly emerges. This pattern is deliberately designed to communicate the central concerns of the play more forcibly.

IMAGES OF CORRUPTION, DISEASE AND POISON

There are repeated references to **nature gone wild**. This type of imagery is used in the aftermath of Claudius's assumption of the throne. There is a particular emphasis on the notion of weeds invading a garden:

- Note the reference to the world as an 'unweeded garden' (I. ii. 135)
- Hamlet tells his mother: 'do not spread the compost on the weeds to make them ranker' (III. iv. 151–2).
- The ghost uses similar imagery to incite Hamlet to act:

> And duller should'st thou be than the fat weed
> That rots itself in ease on Lethe wharf,
> Would'st thou not stir in this.
>
> (I. v. 33–5)

Shakespeare is using the images of the unchecked growth of weeds, and uncontrolled vegetation, as a metaphor for the corruption of the state of Denmark under the rule of Claudius. **Poison images** are also used throughout the play to emphasise the unnatural and untimely deaths that have occurred, or are about to occur; and to illustrate the unhealthy state of the body politic in Denmark.

- The elder Hamlet has been murdered by means of a poison being administered to his 'mildew'd ear' (III. iv. 64).
- The Ghost describes how he was poisoned, emphasising in graphic terms the spreading poison:

> And in the porches of mine ears did pour
> The leprous distilment …
> That swift as quicksilver it courses through
> The natural gates and alleys of the body.
>
> (I. v. 64–7)

There are constant references to sickness and disease throughout the play. These references apply sometimes to specific individuals, sometimes to humankind in general, and sometimes to the state of Denmark or the whole world.

Gertrude speaks of her 'sick soul' (IV. v. 17); Laertes refers to 'the sickness in my heart' and how 'The canker galls the infants of the spring/Too oft before their buttons be disclosed'. Hamlet tells Rosencrantz and Guildenstern that his 'wit's diseas'd', and uses an image of disease to berate and warn his mother in her relations with the current king:

> Lay not that flattering unction to your soul …
> It will but skin and film the ulcerous place,
> Whiles rank corruption, mining all within,
> Infects unseen.
>
> (III. iv. 145–9)

Claudius compares himself to 'the owner of a foul disease' (IV. i. 21), and it is ironic that he sees Hamlet in terms of a disease that must be rooted out when it is he who has infected the state of Denmark:

> Diseases desperate grown
> By desperate appliance are reliev'd,
> Or not at all …
>
> (IV. iii. 9–11)

For Claudius, the cure is to send Hamlet to England: 'For like the hectic in my blood he rages/And thou must cure me …' (IV. iv. 64–5).

All these images of sickness, disease and rottenness make reference to and symbolise the corruption that is at the heart of the state, and the associated evil in humankind that has caused this corruption to occur.

Hamlet describes to Horatio the ease with which subversion can occur, and how human nature can be infected or corrupted by a very small blemish:

> … that these men,
> Carrying, I say, the stamp of one defect …
> His virtues else, be they as pure as grace …
> Shall in the general censure take corruption
> From that particular fault.
>
> (I. iv. 30–6).

Hamlet describes Claudius as 'the canker of our nature' and describes his mother's association with Claudius as one that 'takes off the rose/From the fair forehead of an innocent love,/And sets a blister there' (III. iv. 44–5).

Function of Corruption/Disease/Poison Imagery
- To illustrate the themes of corruption, and good and evil.
- To develop the characterisation and atmosphere of a state in crisis and decline.

ANIMAL IMAGERY

Animal imagery is used particularly to define the relationship between Claudius and Gertrude. The bestial nature of their relationship is constantly suggested by Hamlet through the use of animal imagery.

Hamlet also uses this type of imagery to dehumanise and diminish those he perceives to be allies of the King and those who carry out his instructions. This is particularly to be noted in relation to Polonius. When he meets Polonius after putting on his 'antic disposition' he speaks of the sun breeding 'maggots in a dead dog' (II. ii. 181). He calls Claudius a 'paddock' [toad], a 'bat' and a 'gib' [tomcat] (III. iv. 190), emphasising the animal instincts of Claudius in particular, but also of those who surround him, including Gertrude and even Ophelia.

The way Hamlet ties in the notion of lust to animal imagery in order to emphasise his abhorrence for his mother's and the king's relationship is particularly noteworthy:

> In the rank sweat of an enseamed bed,

Stew'd in corruption, honeying and making love
Over the nasty sty!'

(III. iv. 92–4)

It implies the animal nature of lust. In this same scene Hamlet's disgust for the relationship between Claudius and Gertrude is also contained in the following lines:

Let [not] the bloat King tempt you again to bed;
Pinch wanton on your cheek; call you his mouse …

(III. iv. 183–4).

Function of Animal Imagery

- To define the character of Claudius and his relationship with Gertrude.
- To illustrate the theme of love and to differentiate between love and lust.
- To set the mood of a world without laws (the law of the jungle) created by men without morals.

WAR/BATTLE IMAGERY

This type of imagery is used throughout the play, to suggest the conflict and struggle for supremacy between the forces of good and of evil. This becomes a central concern for Hamlet, who sees the fortress of good being assailed by the forces of evil.

Bernardo will 'assail' Horatio's ears, which are 'fortified' against his story (I. i). Laertes tells Ophelia to 'keep in the rear' of her affection towards Hamlet, 'Out of the shot and danger of desire . . .' (I. iii. 35). Polonius reiterates this notion, advising Ophelia to set her 'entreatments at a higher rate/Than a command to parley . . .' (I. iii. 122–3).

Horatio paints a picture of Denmark preparing for war. He states that the threat of Fortinbras is:

the main motive of our preparations,
The source of this our watch, and the chief head
Of this post-haste and romage in the land.

(I. i. 105–7)

Hamlet uses war imagery to indicate and steel his intentions to upset Claudius's plans to have him killed and also to overthrow Claudius:

> For 'tis the sport to have the engineer
> Hoist with his own petar; and 't shall go hard
> But I will delve one yard below their mines
> And blow them at the moon.
>
> (III. iv. 207–10).

Claudius speaks in warlike terms of the slander that may fall on his name through Hamlet's deeds:

> [Slander,] whose whisper o'er the world's diameter,
> As level as the cannon to his blank [target]
> Transports his poisoned shot—may miss our name
> And hit the woundless air.
>
> (IV. v. 40–4).

When Claudius sees the mad Ophelia he conveys his feelings to Gertrude in the imagery of battle: 'O Gertrude, Gertrude/When sorrows come, they come not single spies/But in battalions.' (IV. v. 77–8).

Functions of War/Battle Imagery

- Reflects and illustrates the theme of good and evil.
- Creates a mood of disorder and turbulence.
- Communicates the sense of the violence brought about by Claudius's murder of his brother and usurpation of his throne.

CLOTHING, DISGUISE AND ACTING IMAGERY

These images are used to reflect the themes of hypocrisy, and appearance and reality. Hamlet is aware of the discrepancy between what seems and what is. He is constantly preoccupied with lifting the veil of appearance. He is aware that his black clothes are '. . . but the trappings and the suits of woe' (I. ii. 86), outward signs of sadness that anybody could wear even if they did not feel grief—'. . . they are actions that a man might play' (I. ii. 84).

Polonius uses a clothing image in his instructions to Reynaldo '. . . and there put on him/What forgeries you please . . .' (II. i. 19–20); and in this instance such imagery reflects the hypocritical character of Polonius. In Act IV scene vii, Hamlet informs Claudius in his letter that he has returned to Denmark 'naked': this could hint that he has despatched Claudius's two assassins, Rosencrantz and Guildenstern, but it also indicates that he has shed his 'antic disposition' and that he is stripped down to his true self.

When Hamlet discovers Yorick's skull in the graveyard episode, it begins to symbolise for him man in his essence—dust. Hamlet sees man's life as a futile attempt to disguise this fact. Hamlet has realised this when he tells Ophelia, 'God hath given you one face, and you make yourselves another . . .' (III. i. 142–3).

In his encounter with Ophelia in Act V scene I, Hamlet recognises the futility of life's pretences in:

> Now get you to my Lady's chamber,
> And tell her, let her paint an inch thick,
> To this favour she must come.
> (V. i. 183–5).

Polonius, in his advice to Laertes, tells him that '. . . the apparel oft proclaim the man . . .' (I. iii. 72) and that we judge people by appearance. He restates this sentiment to Claudius when he sets Ophelia to spy on Hamlet:

> 'Tis too much proved, that which devotion's visage
> And pious action we do sugar o'er
> The Devil himself …
> (III. i. 47–9)

Claudius responds by saying in an aside, 'How smart a lash that speech doth give my conscience!' (III. i. 50).

Acting is also a significant symbol in this play. The players are introduced in Act III and we are made aware of the difference between the players who act so as to reveal man to himself—to 'hold as 'twere the mirror up to nature' (III. ii. 20)—and the other characters who assume their roles for the purposes of concealment. Claudius assumes the role of rightful king; Gertrude of virtuous queen; Hamlet of the mad prince; Reynaldo of a disinterested observer/acquaintance; and finally Laertes and Ophelia as a trap to ensnare Hamlet.

Functions of Clothing/Disguise/Acting Imagery

- To show the lengths people will go to engage in deception.
- To underline the predominance of insincerity in dealings with people.
- To highlight the fundamental need for truth and sincerity in human relations.

NOTE

When you are revising this play, remember that language and imagery do not stand alone: they exist to make the key ideas and themes come alive for the reader or audience. When you are studying the language and images, always remember to examine what they are saying about:

- the character who uses that particular language and/or images
- the themes or main ideas that the playwright wishes to communicate.

KEY QUOTATIONS AND HOW TO USE THEM

Below is a list of quotations arranged according to theme and character. Study where they appear in the play and what exactly they are saying about either a theme or a particular character. These can be used in answering exam-style questions. It may also help to add your own choice of quotations to this list.

HAMLET'S CHARACTER

'I have that within which passes show.' (Act I, scene ii)

'How weary, stale, flat, and unprofitable/Seem to me all the uses of this world!' (Act I, scene ii)

''Tis an unweeded garden/That grows to seed; things rank and gross in nature/Possess it merely.' (Act I, scene ii)

'. . . his will is not his own;/For he himself is subject to his birth.' (Act I, scene iii)

'I do not set my life at a pin's fee.' (Act I, scene iv)

'As I perchance hereafter shall think meet/To put an antic disposition on.' (Act I, scene v)

'Hamlet's transformation.' (Act II, scene ii)

'My too much changed son.' (Act II, scene ii)

'I am but mad north-north-west. When the wind is southerly I know a hawk from a handsaw.' (Act II, scene ii)

'A dull and muddy-mettled rascal.' (Act II, scene ii)

'But I am pigeon-livered and lack gall/To make oppression bitter.' (Act II, scene ii)

'Thus conscience does make cowards of us all.' (Act III, scene i)

'O, what a noble mind is here o'erthrown!/The courtier's, soldier's, scholar's, eye, tongue, sword,/Th' expectancy and rose of the fair state/The glass of fashion, and the mould of form,/Th' observed of all observers, quite, quite down.' (Act III, scene i)

'Let me be cruel, not unnatural;/I will speak daggers to her, but use none.' (Act III, scene ii)

'For this same lord,/I do repent; but heaven hath pleas'd it so,/To punish me with this, and this with me,/That I must be their scourge and minister. (Act III, scene iv)

'He's lov'd of the distracted multitude.' (Act IV, scene iii)

'The great love the general gender bear him.' (Act IV, scene vii)

'How all occasions do inform against me/And spur my dull revenge.' (Act IV, scene iv)

'O, from this time forth/My thoughts be bloody, or be nothing worth!' (Act IV, scene iv)

'Most generous and free from all contriving.' (Act IV, scene vi)

'This is I,/Hamlet the Dane.' (Act V, scene i)

'I loved Ophelia.' (Act V, scene i)

'There's a divinity that shapes our ends/Rough-hew them how we will.' (Act V, scene i)

'. . . we defy augury. There's a special providence in the fall of a sparrow. If it be now, 'tis not to come; if it be not to come, it will be now; if it be not now, yet it will come: the readiness is all.' (Act V, scene ii)

'His madness is poor Hamlet's enemy.' (Act V, scene ii)

'Now cracks a noble heart. Good-night, sweet prince,/And flights of angels sing thee to thy rest!' (Act V, scene ii)

'For he was likely, had he been put on,/To have prov'd most royally.' (Act V, scene ii)

THE GHOST

'. . . this thing'/'this dreaded sight'/'this apparition' (Act I, scene i)

'In the same figure, like the King that's dead.' (Act I, scene i)

'This bodes some strange eruption to our state.' (Act I, scene i)

'A countenance more in sorrow than in anger.' (Act I, scene ii)

'Thou com'st in such a questionable shape.' (Act I ,scene iv)

'Cut off even in the blossoms of my sin,/Unhous'led, disappointed, unanel'd,/No reckoning made, but sent to my account/With all my imperfections on my head.' (Act I, scene v)

'The spirit that I have seen/May be a devil; and the devil hath power/T'assume a pleasing shape.' (Act II, scene ii)

'This visitation/Is but to whet thy almost blunted purpose.' (Act III, scene iv)

CLAUDIUS'S CHARACTER

'The serpent that did sting thy father's life/Now wears his crown.' (Act I, scene v)

'. . . that incestuous, that adulterate beast.' (Act I, scene v)

'O villain, villain, smiling, damned villain!' (Act I, scene v)

'How smart a lash that speech doth give my conscience!' (Act III, scene i)

'. . . frighted with false fire' (Act III, scene ii)

'O, my offence is rank, it smells to heaven;/It hath the primal eldest curse upon't,/ A brother's murther!' (Act III, scene iii)

'I am still possess'd/Of those effects for which I did the murther —/My crown, mine own ambition, and my queen.' (Act III, scene iii)

'My words fly up, my thoughts remain below/Words without thoughts never to heaven go.' (Act III, scene iii)

'. . . like a mildew'd ear/Blasting his wholesome brother.' (Act III, scene iv)

'A cutpurse of the empire and the rule.' (Act III, scene iv)

'For like the hectic in my blood he rages.' (Act IV, scene iii)

'Revenge should have no bounds.' (Act IV, scene vii)

'. . . thou incestuous, murd'rous, damned Dane.' (Act V, scene ii)

GERTRUDE'S CHARACTER

'Frailty, thy name is woman!' (Act I, scene ii)

'. . . my most seeming-virtuous queen.' (Act I, scene v)

'Leave her to heaven,/And to those thorns that in her bosom lodge/To prick and sting her.' (Act I, scene v)

'O most pernicious woman.' (Act I, scene v)

'The lady doth protest too much, methinks.' (Act III, scene ii)

'Such an act/That blurs the grace and blush of modesty;/Calls virtue hypocrite; takes off the rose/From the fair forehead of an innocent love,/And sets a blister there; makes marriage vows/As false as dicers' oaths.' (Act III, scene iv)

'Thou turn'st mine eyes into my very soul,/And there I see such black and grained spots/As will not leave their tinct.' (Act III, scene iv)

'To my sick soul, as sin's true nature is . . .' (Act IV, scene v)

'She's so conjunctive to my life and soul/That, as the star moves not but in his sphere,/I could not but by her.' (Act IV, scene vii)

OPHELIA'S CHARACTER

'You speak like a green girl.' (Act I, scene ii)

'. . . poor Ophelia/Divided from herself and her fair judgment.' (Act IV, scene v)

'Who is this they follow?/And with such maimed rites? This doth betoken/The corse they follow did with desp'rate hand/Fordo it own life. 'Twas of some estate.' (Act V, scene i)

'Her death was doubtful.' (Act V, scene i)

POLONIUS

'Neither a borrower nor a lender be;/For loan oft loses both itself and friend.' (Act I, scene iii)

'. . . brevity is the soul of wit . . .' (Act II, scene ii)

'I will find/Where truth is hid, though it were hid indeed/Within the centre.' (Act II, scene ii)

'Though this be madness, yet there is a method/in't.' (Act II, scene ii)

'If you call me Jephthah, my lord.' (Act II, scene ii)

'I'll silence me even here./Pray you be round with him.' (Act III, scene iv)

'. . . this counsellor/Is now most still, most secret, and most grave,/Who was in life a foolish prating knave.' (Act III, scene iv)

FORTINBRAS

'. . . young Fortinbras,/Of unimproved mettle hot and full.' (Act I, scene i)

'Led by a delicate and tender prince,/Whose spirit, with divine ambition puff'd,/Makes mouths at the invisible event.' (Act IV, scene iv)

'I do prophesy th'election lights/On Fortinbras. He has my dying voice.' (Act V, scene ii)

FALSE APPEARANCE/DISSIMULATION/DECEIT

'Foul deeds will rise,/Though all the earth o'erwhelm them, to men's eyes.' (Act I, scene ii)

'By indirections find directions out.' (Act II, scene i)

'The play's the thing/Wherein I'll catch the conscience of the King.' (Act II, scene ii)

'I have heard of your paintings too, well enough. God hath given you one face and you make yourselves another.' (Act III, scene i)

'Now get you to my Lady's chamber,/And tell her, let her paint an inch thick,/To this favour she must come.' (Act V, scene i)

EVIL

'Something is rotten in the state of Denmark.' (Act I, scene iv)

'Revenge his foul and most unnatural murder.' (Act I, scene v)

'Why, as woodcock to mine own springe . . . I am justly killed with mine own treachery.' (Laertes, Act V, scene i)

'Of carnal, bloody and unnatural acts;/Of accidental judgments, casual slaughters;/Of deaths put on by cunning and forc'd cause;/And, in this upshot, purposes mistook/Fall'n on th' inventors' heads.' (Act V, scene ii)

'. . . to suffer/The slings and arrows of outrageous fortune.' (Act III, scene i)

REVENGE/VENGEANCE

'Revenge his foul and most unnatural murder.' (Act I, scene v)

'The time is out of joint. O cursed spite/That ever I was born to set it right!' (Act I, scene v)

'But my revenge will come.' (Act IV, scene vii)

'Revenge should have no bounds.' (Act IV, scene vii)

KINGSHIP/POWER

'There's such divinity doth hedge a king/That treason can but peep to what it would,/Acts little of his will.' (Act IV, scene v)

'The cess of majesty/Dies not alone, but like a gulf doth draw/What's near it with it.' (Act III, scene iii)

'Between the pass and fell incensed points/Of mighty opposites.' (Act V, scene ii)

IRONIC REMARKS OR STATEMENTS

'This above all—to thine own self be true,/And it must follow, as the night the day,/Thou canst not then be false to any man.' (Act I, scene ii)

'Ay, springes to catch woodcocks.' (Act I, scene iii)

'. . . that I, with wings as swift/As meditation or the thoughts of love,/May sweep to my revenge.' (Act I, scene v)

'Now could I drink hot blood,/And do such bitter business as the day/Would quake to look on.' (Act III, scene ii)

'I'll silence me even here./Pray you be round with him.' (Act III, scene iv)

SUMMARY OF SOLILOQUIES AND ASIDES

Study the note on the use of the Soliloquy on page 4.

Remember that Shakespeare makes use of the soliloquy to give us the audience a deeper insight into a character, other than what we have learned from their conversations with different people. A soliloquy is an insight into the soul and mindset of that character.

For each soliloquy, examine the following points.

- Where in the play does this soliloquy occur?
- What do we learn about the person from the soliloquy?
- What images are used and what function do they serve?
- What does this soliloquy tell us about the action/plot?
- Are there certain themes expressed in the soliloquy?

HAMLET

Soliloquy One: Act I, scene ii, lines 129–160

- This occurs just after the coronation ceremony in which Claudius has assumed the throne of Denmark.
- Hamlet feels a revulsion for the world, considering it an 'unweeded garden'. He feels suicidal, but believes in the law of God that forbids this. He is disgusted by his mother's hasty marriage to Claudius.
- Images: weeds and corruption. Classical images, referring to his father: 'a Hyperion to a satyr'; Hercules.
- Plot: We learn that Claudius and Gertrude were married within a month of Old Hamlet's death.
- Themes: bitterness against life; suicide; frail womanhood; incest; marriage.

Soliloquy Two: Act I, scene v, lines 92–112

- This comes immediately after Hamlet has met the Ghost and heard the details of Claudius's murder.
- Hamlet is horrified and decides to keep the Ghost's commandment as the only idea in his brain
- Images: 'smiling, damned villain', highlights Claudius's lack of sincerity; 'pernicious woman' refers to Gertrude's evil action in marrying Claudius and thereby committing incest.

- Plot: Hamlet decides to keep the Ghost's command foremost in his plan of action.
- Themes: insincerity; a sense of horror at evil committed; evil.

Soliloquy Three: Act II, scene ii, lines 536–94 (the Hecuba Soliloquy)

- The players have arrived at Elsinore and have performed a short play about Hecuba the queen in which they were moved to tears, even though it was only drama.
- Hamlet chastises himself for being slow in carrying out the act of revenge. He also describes himself as a coward, 'pigeon-liver'd', an 'ass'.
- Images: Hamlet uses negative, self-castigatory images about himself and his tardiness: 'dull and muddy-mettled rascal'; 'I am pigeon-liver'd and lack gall/To make oppression bitter.'
- Plot: Hamlet decides to stage a play that night in order to see whether or not the Ghost is authentic (Hamlet thinks the Ghost might be a 'devil'.)
- Themes: cowardice; acting/drama; equivocation/double-dealing.

Soliloquy Four: Act III, scene i, lines 56–90

- This takes place shortly before the Nunnery Scene.
- In this soliloquy, 'To be, or not to be', Hamlet appears a very speculative and philosophical character. One critic, on the basis of this soliloquy, described him as a 'Prince of philosophical speculators'.
- Images: 'slings and arrows of outrageous fortune'; 'shuffled off this mortal coil'; 'whips and scorns of time'; 'The undiscovered country, from whose bourn/No traveller returns'.
- Plot: Hamlet is condemning himself for his inaction and his 'conscience'.
- Themes: life and death; life after death; suffering and injustice; cowardice.

Soliloquy Five: Act III, scene ii, lines 369–80

- Hamlet has just staged 'The Mousetrap' and managed to prove Claudius's guilt.
- Hamlet declares that he could drink 'hot blood', carry out a powerful revenge plan.
- Images: 'witching time of night'; drinking hot blood; speak daggers, but use none.
- Plot: Hamlet announces his intention of confronting his mother with her guilt now that he has successfully proved his uncle's guilt.
- Themes: evil-doing; revenge; hypocrisy.

Soliloquy Six: Act III, scene iii, Lines 73–95

- Hamlet sees the king praying in his chapel and decides it is a perfect opportunity to carry out his revenge, but changes his mind again.
- Hamlet's reasoning process here shows him to be very callous and unchristian—he wants Claudius damned in hell.
- Images: damned and black as hell; 'This physic but prolongs thy sickly days'.
- Plot: Hamlet decides to catch his uncle in an act that will damn his soul to hell, and that will constitute a fitting revenge plan for Hamlet.
- Themes: revenge; evil and damnation; sin

Soliloquy Seven: Act IV, scene iv, lines 31–66

- Young Fortinbras is passing through Denmark on his way to capture a small tract of land in Poland. Hamlet, who is on his way to England in the company of Rosencrantz and Guildenstern, wonders what Fortinbras is doing.
- Hamlet again chastises himself for his lack of action as he compares himself with Fortinbras. He condemns himself for too much thought and not enough action
- Images: 'dull revenge'; an eggshell; a 'mother stain'd'.
- Plot: Hamlet resolves immediately to do something about avenging his father.
- Themes: excessive speculation/thinking; war; honour; revenge.

CLAUDIUS

Aside: Act III, scene i, lines 50–4

- Claudius and Polonius are using Ophelia as a bait to trap Hamlet into revealing what lies at the heart of his change in temperament and behaviour. Polonius has been preaching about hypocrisy and how often we 'sugar o'er/The devil himself' in the false way we act.
- For the first time in the play we realise that Claudius has a conscience and a sense of sin and guilt.
- Images: painting and the prostitute (these themes recur repeatedly in the play)—'the harlot's cheek', 'plastering art', 'painted word'.
- Themes: hypocrisy; false appearance; guilt.

Soliloquy One: Act III, scene iii, lines 36–72

- This occurs immediately after the staging of the play 'The Mousetrap', in which all the details of the murder were enacted before the whole court. Claudius is on his knees in his private chapel attempting to pray and to repent of his crimes.

- Claudius feels the weight of guilt: he does possess a conscience and has faith in God. He is also driven by a lust for power and for Gertrude, so there is a strong internal struggle here between his sense of guilt and his ambition to remain king.
- Images: 'my offence is rank'; 'My crown, mine own ambition, and my queen'; 'limed soul'.
- Plot: the development of the plot is based on Claudius's internal state. All action will be governed by the outcome of his struggle with his conscience and with his creator.
- Themes: personal freedom; sense of sin and guilt/repentance; personal ambition/lust for power.

GERTRUDE

Aside: Act IV, scene v, lines 17–20

- The queen has just heard about Ophelia's madness and how she is spreading rumours in the kingdom about Claudius.
- We learn that Gertrude feels guilty and in sin because of her behaviour with Claudius.
- Images: 'sick soul'; 'toy'; 'spills itself'.
- Themes: guilt and sin.

SOME KEY SITUATIONS

The following key situations from *Hamlet* can be useful if you are using this play to answer a comparative question. There are four key situations selected here and under each we look at the headings that come up every year in the comparative section. Under each heading is a list of ideas that could be examined in a comparative essay.

THE PRAYER SCENE, ACT III, SCENE III

Genre

- The use of situational irony—the king seems to be a holy man repenting of his crime and making his peace with God—but the reality is different: his ambition supersedes his capacity to repent.
- Images: 'rank'; 'thick with brother's blood'; limed soul'; 'heart with strings of steel'; 'damned and black as hell'; 'this physic but prolongs thy sickly days'.
- Examine the two soliloquies in this section—Claudius's and Hamlet's—and study the examples of irony in both.

Cultural Context

- The setting—inside a small chapel in the palace of Elsinore.
- The suggestion that the king is a Catholic—he speaks very clearly about sin, guilt, Cain's murder in the Bible, and damnation.
- The power inherent in kingship—how many subjects depend on the king.

General Vision and Viewpoint

- The idea inherent in the play that each character is forced to face the fact that they must answer for their deeds in this world and in the next.
- Part of Shakespeare's general vision and viewpoint deals with the notion of punishment for sins committed; in the Ghost's comments, and here in Hamlet's and Claudius's soliloquies.
- Freedom to act or not to act is an integral part of the general vision of the play. Here this is dramatised vividly in the king's speech and in Hamlet's soliloquy.

Theme/Issues

- Sin/hell/damnation.
- Kingship/power.
- Repentance.
- Freedom.

THE NUNNERY SCENE, ACT III, SCENE I

Genre

- The dialogue used; the use of irony, puns, satire, etc.
- Images: 'paintings', 'noble mind . . . o'erthrown', bells jangled out of tune, 'Blasted with ecstasy'.
- Ophelia's speech of lament and the cruel ironies here.

Cultural Context

- The notion underlying a nunnery—does Hamlet mean a brothel or a convent?
- Hamlet seems to suggest to Ophelia that the women of the day were characterised by mere false appearance, by changing their faces with 'painting'.
- The particular status and situation of the young prince is exemplified clearly in Ophelia's speech about the 'courtier', the 'soldier', and the 'glass of fashion'. The prince at that time must have been a model of many virtues.

General Vision and Viewpoint

- Part of the general vision and viewpoint in this tragedy seems to rest on the notion of how women were mere pawns in the male-dominated world.
- Shakespeare stresses repeatedly in the play the notion of duplicity in human dealings, and this applies in particular to the case of the women characters in the play. (It also seems to form a part of the general vision of the play.)
- There is a strong sense of the sufferings caused by madness and by deceit in human relations—another aspect of the general vision that is shown here in this section.

Themes/Issues

- Frail womanhood.
- Madness.
- Honesty/false appearance.

THE FINAL SCENE—THE DUEL BETWEEN HAMLET AND LAERTES

Genre

- The dramatic duel with the poisoned sword and the poisoned wine.
- The number of dead people on the stage and the arrival of Fortinbras with his assumption of power.
- The use of irony and dramatic dialogue.

Cultural Context

- The type of entertainment in the royal courts at that time—fencing and duelling.
- The 'silly' courtier Osric and his role in Elsinore.
- The arrival of another political power (Fortinbras) and his accession to the throne of Denmark.

General Vision and Viewpoint

- There seems to be an underlying idea that a divine providence overrules the events and the lives of the characters in the play—this general vision is evident in the concluding events.
- Characters are free in their actions but have to answer for the consequences of these actions. This idea is borne out in the final scene.
- Death is an inevitable part of life, and death seems to triumph over all types of corruption. From the appearance of the Ghost right through to the concluding scene, this theme is part of the general vision of the play.

Themes/Issues

- Death.
- Violence.
- Justice.
- Kingship.

HOW TO STUDY THIS PLAY

At Higher Level English it is important to be able to analyse the type of play you are working with, and to understand fully the motivations of the various characters presented at every stage in the plot.

Since *Hamlet* is a tragedy, it is important to study the notes on Shakespearean tragedy and to note the particular aspects of the play that make it tragic. In particular, you need to form your own opinions on the main hero, or main protagonist. Make sure you understand clearly what is the **tragic flaw** in Hamlet and can identify this throughout the play by pinpointing certain events and quotations.

First get to grips with the story and the plot. Try to create a graph or map of the action and the subsequent consequences of all action taken.

After you have come to an understanding of the plot and of what contributes to the main action in the play, begin to study the main characters. The characters give rise to the action, and also to the main issues or themes that are dealt with in the play. In your analysis of the character of each protagonist, look at what other people say about them.

In Shakespearean drama, we can also learn a lot about characters through analysing their asides and/or soliloquies. Shakespeare gives Hamlet many soliloquies, through which we can gain an insight into his frame of mind and what motivates him in thought and in action. Similarly, Claudius has several soliloquies, which serve to give us a deeper understanding of his nature and motivations.

Certain images can give us another insight into a character. Images can help to paint a picture of the type of person a character is and what motivates their actions. Take, for example, the Ghost's reference to Claudius as 'that incestuous, that adulterate beast', and to Gertrude as 'my most seeming-virtuous queen'. These images make some powerful statements about the situation in the play. At that time, the act of marrying one's brother's wife was taken as an act of incest. Claudius and Gertrude must also have committed adultery, while Gertrude acts the part of a woman of virtue and goodness.

It can help to write out a list of images that are used in relation to a character and to use them for your answers. Try to form your own judgments about the different characters and their behaviour in the play. While these notes can help to some degree, your own personal analysis and judgment are more valuable and certainly help towards gaining that higher mark in your exam.

Having come to understand the characters, begin to look at the main ideas or themes that are expressed through the events of the play. Form your own opinions about these ideas and link them with the motivations that govern the behaviour of the different people in the play. Many times both imagery and language will give you clues to the main ideas in the play and to the statements being made by the playwright on those ideas.

It is not enough just to extract the central ideas of the play: you must go further and see what point or what statement is being made about each issue or theme.

Take some important scenes and study them in more detail.

• Examine what dramatic function each scene has in the overall structure of the play.
• How does the scene contribute to the subsequent action in the play?
• Does the scene highlight any new features of characters through asides or soliloquies?
• Has the scene made a statement (or statements) on themes or issues? And if so, what is this statement?

Write out your own list of quotations and learn them. Be able to weave them naturally and fluidly into your answers.

Practise writing answers to questions asked in previous exams. Try to get to the stage where you are writing your answer in the same time that you will have in your exam, which is about fifty minutes.

HOW TO ANSWER EXAM-STYLE QUESTIONS

O
ne of the biggest difficulties in answering exam-style questions on any area in
literature, and especially on Shakespeare's plays, is to avoid simply telling the
story. Questions at Higher Level English presuppose that you have an intimate
knowledge of the text, and therefore it is not necessary to recount exactly what happens at
every stage. Besides, exams are testing your ability to extract certain information and to
evaluate it in the light of a question. The Higher Level question also tests your ability to
form your own judgments about issues and character motivation. Knowing what
information to leave out can often be as important as knowing what points and what
quotes you need to use.

When answering exam-style questions on the Shakespearean play it is important to
look very closely at every word in the question and at the *way the question is phrased*. Take,
for example, a question such as 'Discuss the dramatic significance of Fortinbras in the play
Hamlet.' This question is not asking you to write about the character of Fortinbras: it is
asking about his *role* in the dramatic structure or the plot of the play and what exactly is
his purpose. A question like this demands that you think a bit about his function, what
part he is playing and the significance of that role or part for the rest of the characters and
the plot.

Simply jotting down all the notes and all the quotations or points you know about the
character of Fortinbras will not be enough to gain that A mark that you would like. Spend
some time thinking about what he does and says in the play, and what you think might be
the purpose of the playwright in constructing him as he has. Reflect also on the way he
speaks and the type of language he uses in the play, and what that is telling us in the
context of this tragic drama.

Gathering quotations that have some relation to the question can be a helpful way of
getting started on a question. You can then build arguments based on these quotations.

Remember that when you make a point about the question in your answer it is
important to support it by using a quotation. Quotations that you use must be commented
on or supported. Don't just plant quotations on the page for purposes of decoration. Every
quotation you use must have a bearing on the question asked, and must be backed up by
your own personal comment or evaluation.

Before you introduce a quotation use a comma or colon and then put inverted commas around the quote; for example, 'Revenge his foul and most unnatural murder.' The full stop or comma normally goes *inside* the closing inverted comma, if the quotation is a complete sentence: otherwise put it outside the inverted comma.

Your answer should be about three or four pages in length. Remember to structure your answer into paragraphs—these can vary in length. Make sure that each paragraph is advancing your argument and is making some point about your question. Before constructing any paragraph, think about the following points.

- What relation has this paragraph to the question asked?
- How is this paragraph linked with the preceding paragraph?
- Have I used a quotation to support the point made in the paragraph?

Avoid the tendency to leave your answer in mid-argument or mid-air. Bring your answer to a logical end and round it off by writing a short but clear conclusion. Your conclusion does not have to be long, but it is the last impression left on your examiner so it should be a good one. You can restate the points you have made and maybe refer again to the question, showing how you stand on it. If you conclude with a quotation, remember you must have commented on its significance.

SOME COMMON MISTAKES

1. Not answering the question.
2. Too much unfocused narrative; failure to mention the actual terms of the question.
3. Answer reveals poor or incorrect knowledge of the play.
4. Failure to support answers with suitable quotations or references to the play.
5. Part or all of the answer is irrelevant.
6. Answer contains padding to make it look longer. This will be penalised.
7. Answer is poorly structured and lacks organisation.
8. Ideas are badly expressed.
9. Answer is too short.
10. Students answer both alternatives. This is a waste of precious time, as only one alternative counts.

TIPS AND HINTS

1. Know the play thoroughly and be able to quote at will.
2. Read the question carefully more than once.

3. Underline the key words in the question.

4. Ensure that you answer all parts of the question.

5. Write in paragraphs. State your point, develop it and support it with quotations and/or reference to the play.

6. Write at least three pages.

7. Be careful not to stray from the question into irrelevance.

8. Avoid waffle or padding. This will not fool the experienced examiners who mark your papers.

9. Remember, you have fifty minutes to write your answer. Do not exceed this time.

10. Understand clearly the various changes within characters as the plot develops.

CRITERIA FOR ASSESSMENT

Below is an outline of how your exam question is marked. Study the points carefully and keep them in mind when you are answering exam-style questions.

Each question is assessed under the following headings:

Clarity of Purpose: Engagement with the set task (e.g. relevance, focus, originality, freshness, clear aim, understanding of genre).

Coherence of Delivery: Ability to sustain the response over the entire answer.

Where appropriate: continuity of argument, sequencing, management of ideas, choice of reference, use of examples, engagement with texts, control of register and shape, creative modelling.

Efficiency of Language Use: Management and control of language to achieve clear communication. (E.g. vocabulary, syntax, sentence patterns, paragraph structure, punctuation appropriate to the register, use of lively interesting phrasing, energy, style, fluency appropriate to the task.)

Accuracy of Mechanics: Spelling, grammar (e.g. appropriate levels of accuracy in spelling, grammatical patterns appropriate to the register).

The marking scheme is:

- Clarity of Purpose (P): 18 marks.
- Coherence of Delivery (C): 18 marks.
- Efficiency of Language Use (L): 18 marks.
- Accuracy of Mechanics (M): 6 marks.

Be sure to keep the criteria for assessment in mind when you are answering exam questions.

SAMPLE QUESTIONS AND ANSWERS

The following questions are taken from past Leaving Cert exam papers. In order to gain the maximum benefit from the sample answers, attempt the question yourself first and see how you would structure your answer and what ideas you would use. Then compare your answer with the sample and see what aspects you might have missed.

Each answer is marked according to the Leaving Cert guide, under P (purpose), C (coherence), L (Language) and M (mechanics).

You could try reading the answers and marking them yourself, remembering to focus on the criteria:

- Purpose: has the actual question been answered, or is there a lot of unfocused narrative?
- Coherence: has the answer been sustained through each paragraph right up to the conclusion? Examine the links made between paragraphs, and between the sentences in each paragraph.
- Language: has the correct use of language been made in the answer, together with appropriate quotation?
- Mechanics: are there errors in grammar and spellings?

Question

'The struggle between Hamlet and Claudius is a fascinating one.'
Discuss this statement, supporting your answer by reference to the play *Hamlet*. (2001)

Answer

This statement is undoubtedly true. The struggle and varying changes within the relationship throughout this play is indeed a fascinating and intriguing one, which is sustained right through to the end of this play. At no stage do we witness a cessation to this struggle between these two 'mighty opposites' in the play. Claudius and Hamlet stand at the centre of the plot and all their actions govern the events that ensue. Both characters are portrayed as powerful people in their own different ways, and the struggle between them is compelling and truly fascinating.

The initial encounter in the play between Hamlet and Claudius occurs just after Claudius has explained the reason why he has married his brother's wife so speedily within the wake of his brother's death. When Claudius tries to address his nephew peaceably, Hamlet treats him with a strong sense of contempt and bitterness. He answers him in ironic and ambiguous puns telling him he is 'a little more than kin and less than kind'. From the outset there is a hostility and tension inherent in the relationship between these two leading protagonists which makes this both a riveting and fascinating play to read and to watch on stage.

Throughout the earlier part of the play we find Claudius and Hamlet playing a game of cat and mouse with each other, each seeking the truth about the other, while concealing the truth about what they themselves know. When the play opens, Claudius's crime is hidden from everyone: it is only the Ghost's revelation that brings this hidden matter to light and then only to Hamlet. From then on, Hamlet himself is concerned, by means of his assumption of an 'antic disposition', at once to keep his knowledge to himself and to watch Claudius, from his safely distanced position as 'madman', for signs of guilt.

In this continuous opposition between the two main characters, the audience's interest is sustained on a high level of excitement and fascination because Shakespeare has taken a lot of trouble to paint these two people vividly, and make them splendid and realistic portraits of humankind. Each of these two men are distinctly different, each are powerful men described aptly as 'mighty opposites' whose power and strength contribute to sustaining a fascinated response from the audience at every stage. Both men are totally different, but both are realistically drawn and manage to influence a lot of people in powerful ways. Claudius is a natural leader of men, just like Hamlet, but in a different way. Claudius has no qualms about telling lies and misleading people whereas Hamlet is deeply sensitive to corruption.

From the outset Shakespeare depicts this struggle between both men in terms of not only physical strength, but also on the level of a moral battle. These men possess a power of virtues and strengths and the combination between both result in some very exciting and dramatic encounters. Take for example Hamlet's determination to expose the conscience of his uncle by staging 'The Mousetrap' play. He manages to keep it a secret and arrange that everyone will be present that night to see the whole details of the murder enacted before their eyes. Hamlet's clever strategy to position himself and Horatio in such a way so as to watch his uncle's reaction to the drama is truly inspiring and fascinating. And so is Claudius's reaction when in anger and fright he begins to call out loud for lights, 'Give me some light—away!', and hurriedly leaves the room. This tension is electric and indeed fascinating to watch in a performance.

We are also exposed to another instance of keen dramatic conflict between both men, in the situation where the unwitting Claudius, struggling to repent in his private chapel, is witnessed by Hamlet. Here Hamlet, on encountering his uncle on his knees in prayer, initially thinks that 'Now I might do it pat, now he is praying.' On further reflection, Hamlet realises that this would not be revenge but a simple reward to his uncle to send him to heaven, 'When he is fit and seasoned for his passage.' Hamlet decides to catch his uncle in an act of damnation where his soul will kick at heaven. Meanwhile to an audience this scene is truly powerful, as we realise the truth about Claudius's interior state of mind, 'My words fly up, my thoughts remain below./Words without thoughts never to heaven go.' Claudius is no more near heaven and salvation than he was before he entered the chapel.

This conflict between the two men intensifies, as Claudius, unwilling to relinquish the fruits of his crime—his crown, his ambition and his queen—becomes more ruthlessly immersed in plotting and evil-doing. Each of the two men in his own way knows the stakes are high, and knows his individual life is endangered by the other. And so each sustains gigantic and marathon efforts towards self-preservation, and in the case of Hamlet, towards struggling to expose the corruption at the heart of Denmark's throne: 'now could I drink hot blood/And do such bitter business as the day/Would quake to look on.' All action and character motivation is speedy, unexpected and dramatic, and ensures that at every stage the audience's attention is captured and held fascinated at the twists and turns of this powerful piece of drama.

So the struggle between the two men develops and changes as the plot unfolds. It becomes an intense psychological battle with one man trying to guess his opponent's next move. Claudius is determined to deal with Hamlet's threat of exposure, telling his leading courtiers how 'we will fetters put upon this fear/Which now goes too free-footed.' This struggle is almost like a crime movie or detective story, where the pace is electric and swift, the plot is action-packed, and where characters battle with one another at every stage. All of which renders the action truly dramatic and fascinating for an audience.

The fact that the action is centred on the plotting of one family also contributes to the power and excitement of this drama. Every member of the family is involved, and each knows the other's moves very well. After the nunnery scene Claudius knows fully that Hamlet's problem is not related to Ophelia, 'Love? His affections do not that way tend.' Claudius is a man of action who knows his nephew's nature very well. The fact that Hamlet's uncle and mother are deeply involved in the action of this drama renders it electrifying at times and keeps an audience rooted to their seat, thus making it a terrific play.

From the exposure of the king right through to the conclusion of this exciting drama, the manoeuvres of both men provide some thrilling drama for an audience. Claudius's moves from now on in the play are directed towards removing Hamlet out of danger to himself, 'Diseases desperate grown/By desperate appliance are reliev'd,/Or not at all.' Ironically, the king who attained his throne through poisoning his own brother begins to use disease imagery to highlight the danger that Hamlet poses to his life: 'like a hectic in my blood he rages'.

Claudius's ability to keep his mind clear and retain a strong sense of self-assurance and calmness in the face of the huge threats posed by his nephew certainly contributes to the increasing intrigue and excitement of this play. At no stage does Claudius manifest any regret or cowardice. His cunning ability to manipulate the weak Laertes in a corrupt duel with the murder of Hamlet at the centre is another factor that sustains the suspense of the drama here.

The attention of the audience is held right through to the final denouement when Hamlet, in a rage on discovering that Claudius has plotted to murder him with a poisoned sword, forces the king to drink the poison while at the same time stabbing him and shouting, 'thou incestuous, murd'rous, damned Dane.'

It can certainly be stated that the struggle between these two men is a very exciting contest made up of a battle of wits, powerful language and dialogue, together with very exciting and dramatic incidents. It is a struggle that is sustained from beginning to end in this superb play, and ensures that the audience's attention is never lost.

P: 17/18
C: 16/18
L: 17/18
M: 6/6
Total: 56/60

COMMENTS/POINTS TO NOTE

Refer to the Guide given by the Department of Education on how to answer this question (page 118), and look at the number of different points that can be included in the answer.

This answer has managed to include most of the points taken from the Guidelines given by the Department of Education on page 118.

The answer focuses on the conflict between Claudius and Hamlet and it makes several points and gives good, clear examples of how this struggle manages to captivate the audience. Notice that the points are supported by relevant quotation and reference from the play.

There is a slight amount of repetition of some points.

Otherwise this adds up to a very good answer.

Question

Choose the scene from Shakespeare's *Hamlet* that in your view was the most dramatic. Discuss your choice, supporting your answer by reference to the play. (Textual support may include reference to a performance.) (2001)

ANSWER

The scene that I consider to be one of the most dramatic in the play Hamlet is the Graveyard Scene which occurs at the end of the play in Act V, scene i. This scene is rich in action and characterisation. It is a scene that is important as it expresses in a very succinct and dramatic way many of the issues that have been developed so far in the drama.

The scene opens with a discussion between two gravediggers who are preparing the burial ground for Ophelia who has committed suicide. Shakespeare deliberately makes these gravediggers play a dual role—they operate as clowns on the one hand, and actual gravediggers on the other. This dual purpose contributes to the power and heightened drama inherent in this scene. In some dramatic productions of this play the clowns/gravediggers are depicted in such a way that an audience is entertained and finds that this scene is rich in humour.

The conversation between these two hinges on Ophelia's death and the question about whether or not she should receive a proper Christian burial, 'Is she to be buried in Christian burial when she wilfully seeks her own salvation?' In their use of ironic statements and humorous puns these clowns or gravediggers not only entertain the audience, but they supply some very rich insights and comments on many of the play's primary themes and issues such as mortality, corruption, equivocation and death.

When Hamlet and Horatio enter, the drama and tone of this scene changes somewhat. It is interesting that Shakespeare has deliberately structured this scene before the concluding scene where most of the main protagonists meet their death. This scene is rich in irony, therefore: where this scene speaks and philosophises about death and the futility of corrupt plotting, the other scene dramatises death and the destruction of evil. With the arrival of Hamlet to the graveyard one of the gravediggers announces how he has been a grave-maker since the day young Hamlet was born. This reference to Hamlet's birth is indeed chillingly ironic given that he will meet with his death in the next scene.

In a recent dramatic production of this play the most powerful piece of dramatic machinery here was the use of props and lighting. The stage was filled with many different skulls, and there was a distinct macabre tone to the backdrop of the setting. Hamlet picks up the skull of Yorick, a court jester whom he knew as a child. As he holds the skull in his hand we begin to see how the tone and atmosphere of the scene changes, and it becomes much more tense and dramatic. Hamlet has been obsessed with the issue of false appearance and hypocrisy throughout the play and here he uses the occasion to condemn false 'paintings' and dissimulation as he chastises this skull with the words, 'Now get you to my Lady's chamber,/And tell her, let her paint an inch thick,/To this favour she must come.' Indeed, for an audience who are exposed to these sharp words the effect is riveting and powerful. We begin to realise the cruel irony inherent in this incident when very soon the dead body of Ophelia is carried into the graveyard.

There is no doubt that the Graveyard Scene is truly one where the drama intensifies at every stage, and this is conveyed in very many different ways by Shakespeare. With the arrival of the dead body of Ophelia the tone and atmosphere again change. When Hamlet looks on from his hiding place in shock at the arrival of the whole court including the King, Queen, and Laertes as they follow the coffin into the graveyard, we realise that the drama has reached a new level of excitement and crisis. Hamlet is initially filled with disbelief and horror at the sudden death of his beloved Ophelia. As the body is lowered into the ground, Laertes makes a powerful leap into the grave, and with a dramatic flourish proceeds to gather his dear sister into his arms, crying out in vengeance against the loss. Immediately without thinking, Hamlet begins to challenge Laertes's histrionics by announcing in dramatic terms, 'This is I,/Hamlet the Dane.' The two men begin to grapple with one another, contributing to the tension of the scene and also filling the place with a great deal of verbal and physical violence. The scene has reached a crucial climax here as we witness the two young protagonists protesting their different loyalties and love for Ophelia. Hamlet dramatically and almost hysterically shouts out how, 'I lov'd Ophelia. Forty thousand brothers/Could not (with all their quantity of love)/Make up my sum.'

Both young men are filled with a profound degree of intense passion and anger, and this confrontation lends a huge power to the drama of this scene. Meanwhile Claudius, who is standing alongside the grave, is horrified at the intrusion and instantly tries to quell Laertes with the words, 'O, he is mad, Laertes.' Claudius is afraid that there may be a murder here beside the grave since Laertes is very hot-headed. As the two men are pulled apart, Claudius moves to caution his wife, telling her to 'set some watch over your son'. Claudius has now distanced himself from any relationship with Hamlet and is simply intent on getting rid of him immediately. As the scene concludes, Claudius consoles Laertes by telling him that he will get his revenge shortly: 'We'll put the matter to the present push.'

There is no doubt that this is one of the most intensely dramatic scenes in the play. Shakespeare uses an enormous variety of richly different characters to dramatise his central themes. It is clear that the skilful juxtapositioning of the Graveyard Scene beside the final scene is a clever tactic on the part of Shakespeare. The Graveyard Scene emphasises the fate of corrupt monarchs, the power of the grave and death, the absurdity of hypocrisy and false behaviour in the face of death.

These very subtle and bitter references to some of the play's central themes are deliberately framed before the final scene which actually dramatises the truth of these reflections spoken about in the graveyard.

Indeed the whole context of a dark and macabre graveyard with its insistent emphasis on the theme of death dramatically reinforces one of the central issues of this play and that is the idea of how death has the last and final triumph in this play. There is no doubt that such reflections will be keenly felt by an audience who in turn will experience all the extraordinary drama of such a powerful scene.

P: 18/18
C: 17/18
L: 17/18
M: 6/6
Total: 58/60

COMMENTS/ POINTS TO NOTE

Look at the Guide given by the Department of Education on how to answer this question (page 119), and look at the number of different points that can be included in the answer.

This is a very good answer on a dramatic scene from the play.

The writer makes reference to many elements that contribute to the drama in the scene. The answer focuses on how this scene links into the play as a whole and how the drama is therefore reinforced.

The answer shows an in-depth knowledge of the scene itself and makes apt use of quotations to sustain the answer at every point.

Perhaps there could be some clearer use of linking devices made between some of the paragraphs in order to develop the points a bit better.

Overall an excellent answer that focuses clearly on the task outlined.

Question

What is your view of the importance of either Gertrude or Ophelia in Shakespeare's Hamlet? Support the points you make by reference to the text.

ANSWER

Ophelia plays a central role in this tragedy even though she is a subordinate character. Her role exists primarily in relation to the central protagonist Hamlet. She is very much in love with him and seemingly he with her until the issue of his father's death occurs. This is a death which happens unexpectedly and changes his attitude to life and to the people around him in a very dramatic way.

Once Hamlet discovers that his uncle may be involved in the murder of his beloved father, all of Hamlet's relationships change including that with Ophelia. From the very beginning of this play, and from our first encounter with Ophelia, we realise that she is young, innocent and very inexperienced in the ways of the world. She belongs to a family where there seems to be no mother figure present. Instead she is in the care of a fairly reckless and fickle brother Laertes, and an old and insidiously deceitful father. These two men seem to be able to manipulate her youth and innocence very easily. From early on in the play she is cautioned by both and told how to behave in her relations with Hamlet. Laertes advises her to safeguard her virtue and not behave recklessly with Hamlet, since 'his will is not his own' and he cannot decide who he will marry. Polonius, her father, warns her about spending too much time in his company and not 'believe his vows', for they are merely trying to beguile her. Ophelia obeys both these two men without placing any obstacle or opposition since her position in a male-dominated world means that she must act as the submissive and docile female.

Ophelia's role therefore is varied. She plays quite a small part yet through her role and position Ophelia highlights the reactions and behaviour of the central protagonist Hamlet in the aftermath of the Ghost's visit. She shows a contemporary audience the submissive and subordinate role of the female in a predominantly patriarchal world.

Shortly after Polonius's words of caution about Hamlet, Ophelia becomes very distressed since Hamlet has come to her with his 'doublet all unbraced,/No hat upon his head, his stockings fouled . . .' and he behaves in an unusual fashion with her. Ophelia clearly is suffering because of this relationship and we realise that perhaps this is another way of Hamlet showing his 'antic disposition' in the play. The role of Ophelia changes as the action develops. Ophelia is an innocent young girl, a 'green girl', who is continually exploited by Claudius and her father Polonius in the service of deception and lies.

Both men decide to use her as a pawn or a means of trapping Hamlet and uncovering what is lying at the essence of his changed temperament and behaviour. In this role, Ophelia again is submissive, acquiescent and simply obeys these two corrupt politicians docilely. When Hamlet meets her alone and innocent with a holy or pious book in her hands he realises immediately that something is amiss, 'Ha, ha! Are you honest?' he asks. Ophelia is used in Act III, scene i as a totally innocent bystander on the part of all of these men who are involved in more subtle political tactics than she would ever be able to comprehend in her naivety and innocence.

As Hamlet lashes out at her vehemently, ordering her to go to a nunnery and not be a breeder of sinners, we the audience begin to feel a profound sympathy for the vulnerable figure of Ophelia who is unwittingly caught in this nasty mesh of lies and deviousness. As Hamlet's anger intensifies, his verbal violence to Ophelia increases, to such a degree that she ends up a broken woman by the conclusion of this scene. At this stage we begin to realise that corruption and evil are beginning to take precedence in the play. As poor Ophelia weeps and laments over what she sees is the tragic change in her beloved Hamlet, lamenting the destruction of a 'noble mind', we the audience begin to realise how Ophelia's role highlights how her innocence and purity have been fully exploited. This indeed forms a dramatic contrast to the insidious corruption inherent in the court of Denmark. In her truly tragic position as a broken woman at the conclusion of this scene, an audience can only have the most profound sympathy for this innocent young woman.

Ironically, Ophelia, while she laments the destruction of Hamlet's fine mental faculties, is the real one who falls victim to madness. Her next appearance in the play will show us a fully mad Ophelia who tragically has become a victim of male exploitation and male selfishness.

It is this ruthlessness on the part of Claudius and Polonius in dealing with the more vulnerable members of society, and in this case with an innocent woman, that draws our sympathy and pity for her plight. Ophelia's sufferings simply intensify from this point onwards while all the time the male protagonists plot and contrive to shield themselves from exposure.

In fact it is in her innocence and purity that we begin to realise the profound contrast with the darker, more devious world of betrayal and murder. She remains an innocent victim caught unawares in a world of real selfishness and a lust for power.

Ophelia's role, then, is as crucial and as complex as that of Gertrude. Like Gertrude, Ophelia is in the play to fail Hamlet, but she is also 'there' for other reasons. Her innocence and idealism acts as a counterbalance to Gertrude's earthly carnality. Ophelia's madness too is related to a central theme of the play, for her real madness contrasts with Hamlet's assumed lunacy. Ophelia too, like Hamlet, must learn to live in a world of evil: in her case, a world where her lover goes mad and kills her father, and a world where she has not a soul in whom she can confide. Ophelia becomes a dramatic symbol of the inadequacy of innocence in a world dominated by corruption at its heart.

Throughout the play Ophelia does indeed enlist both our interest and our sympathy. She symbolises an innocence caught up in a world seething with deceit and corruption. Her tragic but inevitable death is necessary for the full reformation of the state.

P: 17/18
C: 17/18
L: 17/18
M: 6/6
Total: 57/60

COMMENTS/POINTS TO NOTE

Refer to the Guide given by the Department of Education on how to answer this question (page 120), and look at the number of different points that can be included in the answer. This is an answer on the role or function of the character of Ophelia in the play. It is a good answer which makes several points on what her role is in the context of this tragedy.

The answer is sustained throughout and there are many references to her multi-faceted role in the play.

There is a slight amount of repetition in some of the points made, but otherwise it adds up to a very good answer.

Question

'We admire Hamlet as much for his weaknesses as for his strengths.'
Write a response to this view of the character of Hamlet, supporting your points by reference to the text. (2005)

ANSWER

This statement is undoubtedly true in the case of young Hamlet. He is a prince whom we admire very much not only for his great strengths and virtues, which are many, but also for his weaknesses, which govern a lot of the action of this play. When we meet with Hamlet first in the play we realise that he is brooding deeply over something, and we guess it is on account of his father's rather sudden death and the swift remarriage of his mother: 'Within a month,/Ere yet the salt of most unrighteous tears/Had left the flushing in her galled eyes/She married.'

We can sympathise deeply with Hamlet's dilemma from the outset of this play. When Hamlet speaks to Claudius at the beginning we realise that there is an undercurrent of bitterness lying deep within the heart of Hamlet that prevents him from relating properly to his uncle. Likewise, he is sarcastic and angry when he addresses his mother. When we hear his first soliloquy in which he outlines his mindset and attitude to these two people, we begin to realise and understand the reasons for this deep rancour and bitterness. Hamlet feels betrayed by his mother and uncle who have married within a month of burying his dearly beloved father. This is understandable, and even though in his weaknesses he lashes out at both Claudius and Gertrude and later on would like to commit suicide because his world is like an 'unweeded garden' where there are things 'rank and gross in nature', we can still comprehend his plight and sufferings.

Hamlet is represented throughout as a very rich and complex character, a man of profound wit and intelligence whom everyone loves. We learn how Claudius has to be careful in dealing with him because of the great love the 'general gender' have for him. Hamlet is popular, 'loved of the distracted multitude', in spite of all his faults. This is because Hamlet is a very human and humane character. Shakespeare invests Hamlet with a great deal of quick-witted intelligence, together with an ability to sustain clever banter and this indeed is a rich source of enjoyment in the play. Indeed many of his witticisms and clever puns highlight his great intellectual ability and agility.

In addition, Hamlet possesses a deep philosophical capacity that enables him to analyse life and death in so many ways. Take for example the splendid and rich 'To be, or not to be' soliloquy. His loyalty to his friends and in particular his father is also another area that we can understand and enjoy greatly in the character of Hamlet. He is brave and reckless at times and an excellent strategist just like his uncle Claudius.

With the appearance of the Ghost, and his invocation or command to revenge the 'foul and most unnatural murder', Hamlet finds himself confronted with a huge dilemma. He cannot find anyone other than Horatio whom he can confide in and trust, and so he must rely on the 'antic disposition' in order to deal with the situation as best he can. He has to lock all the horror and loathing that he feels on hearing the Ghost's revelations inside in his soul as he does not know who to trust. Hamlet is now faced with the enormous task of revenging himself on Claudius while simultaneously not touching his mother but simply leaving her 'to heaven, And to those thorns that in her bosom lodge/To prick and sting her'. In the face of this enormous challenge Hamlet's character will be tested, and in the testing both his strengths and weaknesses will be manifested clearly.

Hamlet possesses a powerful ability to improvise, for example with the immediate arrival of the players he manages to organise within minutes the staging of a play to trap the conscience of the king. While it is clear that we as an audience are fascinated and thrilled with the character of Hamlet in spite of his flaws and shortcomings, it must be borne in mind that Shakespeare places Hamlet in some morally dubious situations. In these situations Hamlet is forced to perform actions which may be morally questionable and even reprehensible. Take for example the Prayer Scene. Here Hamlet spares the praying Claudius because he believes that if he kills him at that moment his victim will go to Heaven and this would not be an ideal form of revenge, since

Claudius killed the elder Hamlet when the latter was unprepared spiritually for death. So, Hamlet declares, he must wait for an opportunity to take the kind of revenge he assumes his father would have wanted, to catch Claudius in the midst of sin: '. . . about some act/That has no relish of salvation in it/Then trip him, that his heels may kick at heaven/And that his soul may be as damned and black/As hell, whereto it goes'.

No matter how this passage is interpreted, the effect is shocking. Johnson describes it as 'too horrible to be read or uttered'. The attitude expressed by Hamlet here is not the Christian one. When Hamlet uses this type of reasoning we begin to realise that the revenge challenge that has been given to him by the Ghost is becoming a truly gigantic issue in his life.

As for the manner in which Hamlet deals with his two old school friends, there have been many different reactions. Some people argue that when he alters the commission changing his death sentence to theirs that it is a simple act of survival. Others criticise the fact that there is a type of unwarranted brutality about the fact that the two are posted speedily to their deaths with 'no shriving time allowed'.

However, in spite of all of these various and different actions from Hamlet we never lose interest in him, and remain fascinated and intrigued by his character at every stage in this play. Hamlet indeed remains a character who stays in our mind for a long time after we have read the play or seen it performed on stage. There are so many aspects to his character that continue to intrigue us—his complex mode of operating, his ingenuity in the face of deviousness and lies, his ability to improvise and organise a clever way of catching the king, as well as the more negative aspects such as his cruelty to women and his incessant habit of procrastinating and lapsing into self-pity and self-loathing. In spite of all these different aspects to his character Hamlet is a compelling figure who inspires and captures us totally.

P:17/18
C:17/18
L:18/18
M: 6/6
Total:58/60

COMMENTS/POINTS TO NOTE

Refer to the Guide given by the Department of Education on how to answer this question (page 121), and look at the number of different points that can be included in the answer.

This is a very good answer which focuses on the different aspects of Hamlet's character and shows us how he is a figure who continues to entertain and intrigue an audience.

The answer captures all aspects of Hamlet's character and also shows us how he still fascinates and intrigues an audience.

Question

Discuss the statement that Ophelia and Gertrude are weak women, tragic victims of a male-dominated world of corruption and deception. Make reference to or quotation from the play to support your answer.

ANSWER

The moral atmosphere of Denmark is contaminated by Claudius's deed of incest and murder. His ill-gotten wife is a figure of disgust for Hamlet as she is the root of much of his suicidal state and melancholia. In this type of atmosphere it is difficult to know who exactly to trust. People in Denmark seem to be living a lie. The two female characters Ophelia and Gertrude are no exceptions in this respect. They are unwitting victims of corruption and deceit and operate in various ways as weak agents of the male-dominated world of Elsinore. From the outset, Shakespeare makes it very clear that the women in the play are subordinate and weaker than their male counterparts.

Gertrude is married to a murderer and a usurper. She is unaware of this fact. When Hamlet confronts her in the Closet Scene she is amazed and echoes his words in disbelief: 'As kill a king?' However, while she may be ignorant of the true nature of Claudius's deed, she is not guiltless. The ghost informs Hamlet how Claudius 'Won to his shameful lust/The will of my most seeming-virtuous queen.' What is implied here is that Gertrude committed adultery while Old Hamlet lived, and that she was a factor that impelled Claudius to commit the crime of fratricide and murder his own brother while he was sleeping in the garden. Her virtue is 'seeming', it is false, shallow, a sham, a mere pretence. That is why Hamlet treats her with the utmost contempt. For him, she has desecrated womanhood with her deed of incest. In the scene shortly after Claudius has assumed control over Denmark, Gertrude reprimands her son somewhat, questioning why the issue of his father's death should seem to be 'so particular with thee?' Hamlet's way of answering her is simply to lash out vehemently in some very strong words filled with derision and contempt: 'seems, madam, Nay, it is.' What Hamlet seems to be hinting at here is how important truth and reality is and not appearance and seeming. He is saying that anyone can act a part, 'they are actions that a man might play'.

Gertrude, however, is unable to understand this type of reasoning as she is morally blind, and alien from a full knowledge about the man she has just married. It is only after the staging of 'The Mousetrap', and after Hamlet has attacked her in the Closet Scene in an effort to awaken her sense of guilt that at last Gertrude is able to acknowledge she is in sin: 'Thou turn'st mine eyes into my very soul,/And there I see such black and grained spots/As will not leave their tinct.'

Gertrude does not seem to change too much in the play even in the wake of her exposure to the reality of her sin in the Closet Scene. She seems to stand by Claudius right up to the end even protecting him from Laertes's anger and wrath when he discovers his father's speedy death and burial. Gertrude seems to simply fade into the background, unable to do much about her husband's corrupt manoeuvrings. As she drinks in celebration of her son during the duel with Laertes, Claudius watches her drink from the poisoned chalice and simply remains quiet as his instinct towards self-preservation is greater than his love for poor Gertrude. Gertrude dies at the conclusion a weak and tragic victim of the huge corruption and dishonesty that has been a hallmark of Elsinore.

In a different way Ophelia is a weak character who also falls victim to the world of corruption and deceit, all of which is rooted in Claudius. In the Nunnery Scene, she is used as a feeble tool by her father, and by the king. Polonius hypocritically gives her a pious book to read 'to colour her loneliness', and to trap Hamlet into revealing what really underlies the 'antic disposition'. It is this act of false appearance and hypocrisy that causes Claudius to acknowledge his own evil-doing in his first soliloquy.

Claudius and Polonius hide behind the arras. Hamlet immediately realises that she is being used as a scapegoat by these two unscrupulous men. At this stage, his mother's deed has polluted his mind. He cannot see Ophelia in the same light again, because she is a woman like his mother. Besides, she is now being used as a device, and so he lashes out at her in one of his most vehement displays of emotion. He denounces her, repels her, and banishes her to a nunnery so that she will not be a 'breeder of sinners'. As a result of this scene she loses her sanity and eventually commits suicide. Ophelia has destroyed herself while operating as blind instrument serving the selfish interests of both her father and the king.

At the conclusion of the nunnery scene, Ophelia is a broken woman; yet the reaction of Claudius is mere self preservation, 'Madness in great ones must not unwatched go.' Polonius likewise is merely concerned with retaining his political power and shows no concern for her severe emotional disintegration here.

Ophelia is an innocent girl who is set out in striking contrast to Gertrude. Despite the fact that Hamlet is severely cruel to her, and also that Polonius merely uses her as a weak 'green girl', Ophelia still remains a constant lover. The scenes which portray her madness are filled with songs and poems which have lost love as their theme. Her father perverted her love, and much of her tragedy comes from the fact that she is forced to play a role and reject the man she truly loves, only to find herself cruelly rejected by him.

Ophelia is a victim of the corruption that seeps through Denmark on account of the operations of agents such as Claudius the king, and his devious partner Polonius. She is also a victim of Hamlet's disgust with women all of which is rooted in his relationship with his own mother. Gertrude's incest has taken off 'the rose/From the fair forehead of an innocent love,/And sets a blister there'. The innocent love was that between Ophelia and Hamlet, the blister is the incest and Gertrude's association with Claudius. Ironically, Ophelia's innocence helps to destroy her.

There is no doubt, therefore, that these two women are portrayed as weak and subordinate characters who in different ways become tragic victims of the male-dominated world of Elsinore. Both women are weak in their nature and tragically this weakness is manipulated and used in the service of guile, corrupt plotting and selfishness on the part of the males who dominate this world. Both women die in different ways, but both die because of this greed, selfishness and corruption that lies at the heart of Elsinore.

P: 17/18
C: 17/18
L: 16/18
M: 6/6
Total: 56/60

COMMENTS/POINTS TO NOTE

This answer focuses on the roles played by Gertrude and Ophelia in the world of Elsinore, which is dominated by males. The answer maintains a clear focus on the task and sustains the response right through to the conclusion. There are references and quotations from the play to support the points made in the answer. There is a degree of repetition of some key ideas and phrases, which tends to weaken the content slightly. Otherwise a very good attempt at the question.

Question

'Hamlet may have described Polonius as "a wretched rash intruding fool" but he was also a loyal minister and devoted father.' Discuss this statement with quotation from or reference to the play.

ANSWER

Claudius describes Polonius as a man 'faithful and honourable', but it can also be said that behind the façade of the loyal minister and devoted father figure lies a treacherous plotter, with a gravely retarded moral sense. He is undeniably at ease in Claudius's Machiavellian court. This is a court that is full of subterfuge and hidden meaning and 'a little soiled in the working'. In the court of Claudius, hedonism and self-indulgence is rationalised, and conspiracies flourish.

Polonius is the Chief Counsellor of State in Denmark, and operates in the play as the right-hand man of the Claudius the king, seconding his indications at every stage. He is also the father of Laertes and Ophelia who are both young, and whose relationships with some of the characters in the main plot is a central part of this tragedy.

From early on in the play Polonius debases his position of Chancellor by converting it into a means of plotting and spying on other people. He prides himself on his keen powers of detection: 'I will find/Where truth is hid, though it were hid indeed/Within the centre.' He almost believes on principle and as a matter of worldly wisdom the worst about everybody. Shortly after his son Laertes has embarked for France, Polonius sends a messenger to spy on him under the pretext of sending him some money. His underhand and dishonest methods of operating, 'by indirections find directions out', mirror the unbridled self-interest and base behaviour of the court of which he is so integral a part.

He is convinced that Hamlet is trying to seduce Ophelia. This is borne out in the self-revealing way he tells Ophelia to take care or she'll 'tender' him 'a fool'. He orders her to reject Hamlet claiming he is a prince out of 'her star'. Polonius may be acting here as a devoted and concerned father, but his methods and motivation are far removed from those of a dedicated and loving parent. In fact, his commands to his daughter about her relationship with Hamlet play no small part in her later deterioration of character and subsequent madness.

When Ophelia returns to her father distraught at the manner in which Hamlet has behaved towards her, 'with a look so piteous in purport/As if he had been loosed out of hell', the only reaction Polonius has is simple—a dismissive one, 'This is the very ecstasy of love.' Polonius continuously sacrifices the two members of his own family for his own selfish self-advancement. He is a deeply insensitive and self-serving character who just ignores the feelings and judgments of his own children, and in so doing he betrays his responsibilities as a parent and father. He 'looses' his daughter like a prostitute, showing himself reckless of her reputation and safety when service to his king takes precedence over his own family's welfare. Indeed, it is not surprising that as a result, Hamlet compares Polonius to Jephthah, a biblical character who thought he was pleasing God by sacrificing his daughter. Polonius's largely unconditional willingness to exploit and compromise his daughter's innocence and virtue are not the qualities normally associated with a devoted father: and yet paradoxically Polonius will undoubtedly see himself as having acted for his daughter's benefit.

Before his son embarks for France, Polonius spends some time giving him advice on how to survive. The essence of this advice, though sound in a worldly sense, is suggestive of caution and self-interest: 'Give every man thine ear, but few thy voice'; 'rich, not gaudy;/For the apparel oft proclaims the man'. Here again the emphasis is more on public image and reputation than on his son's real moral welfare. His final ironic comment, 'to thine own self be true', only serves to highlight even more dramatically how alien from any real sense of morality and virtue this man is. He spends his time lying and deceiving and yet preaching about sincerity and honesty to his son. It is no surprise, therefore, that he meets his death in an act of deception while intruding into affairs that are none of his business. In this respect he may be termed a 'loyal minister', but it is a loyalty in the service of villainy and deceit, a loyalty that is essentially self-serving. Polonius constantly justifies his 'lawful' spying as being for the 'greater' good of the state of Denmark.

The tedious, long-winded 'intruding fool' may have been the loyal minister that Claudius depicted early on in the play to Laertes: 'The head is not more native to the heart,/The hand more instrumental to the mouth,/Than is the throne of Denmark to thy father.' However, his method of acting and his treatment of people, especially his own two children, only highlight his unscrupulous nature and his lack of respect for people's privacy. His service to a corrupt monarch was a greater motivating force than his loyalty to his two children. Polonius indeed emerges as a 'wretched, rash, intruding fool', who only attained in death those virtues which should have been a hallmark of his character in his life as Chief Counsellor of State, 'most still, most secret, and most grave'. He was a loyal minister in the service of corruption and evil, and tragically a man who served his own interests above that of his two children.

P: 16/18
C: 15/18
L: 15/18
M: 5/6
Total: 51/60

COMMENTS/POINTS TO NOTE

This is an answer to a question based on the character of Polonius in the play. The answer focuses on the different aspects in the question: the fact that Polonius is a 'wretched, rash, intruding fool', and also the fact that he is a loyal minister to the king and a loving father.

The writer disagrees with some aspects of the question and uses references and quotation from the play to support the answer.

The answer is a little short for such a rich question and could focus on giving equal amount of space to the different parts of this question.

Overall, it is a good answer but could be improved by developing some points in greater detail.

The following question is taken from 'Exemplars of Standard' issued by the Department of Education and Science.

Question

'For some people Claudius is a black-hearted villain who is justly punished for the murder of his brother, while for others he is a potentially good king who pays dearly for his past.'

Which of these two views of Claudius would you favour more? Support your discussion by reference to the play. (In your answer you may discuss one or both of the above views of the character.)

ANSWER

'That one may smile, and smile, and be a villain;/At least I'm sure it may be so in Denmark.'

I think that this quote from Hamlet when speaking about Claudius shows that he was a black-hearted villain who is justly punished for the murder of his brother. In my opinion I found Claudius to be a vile character who had no regard for anyone except himself and his main concern was that the crown of Denmark sat on his head. By looking at his relationships with the various characters in the play I think it is easy to see the real Claudius—the villain.

He was insanely jealous of the King Hamlet, his brother, and killed him by pouring poison in his ear while he slept. Although in some cases this one act could be forgiven as a moment of madness it was his premeditated actions throughout the play which confirmed his villainy. In order to gain the vacant throne for himself he seduced King Hamlet's widow Gertrude and married her within a month of his brother's death. He did appear throughout the play to have a genuine affection for Gertrude but the amount of crude sexual references confirm it was more lust. His final treachery towards Gertrude was shown when he made very little attempt to stop her drinking the poisoned chalice which killed her. He had murdered his brother and wife in cold blood.

From the beginning of the play Claudius referred to Hamlet as his son almost as if he had adopted him after his father's death. Everything was fine until Claudius discovered that Hamlet knew that he had killed King Hamlet, and his whole attitude towards Hamlet changed. When speaking to Gertrude, Hamlet was her son and he declared that Hamlet's madness was reason enough to send him to England. He dispatched Hamlet with two servants, Rosencrantz and Guildenstern. They had in their possession a letter which told the King of England to execute Hamlet the minute he reached the country. He was willing to kill his nephew and his wife's son in order to keep his crown and his secret. This shows how evil he was and how calculating he was in this evil. When Hamlet foiled the plan and Rosencrantz and Guildenstern were executed instead, although Claudius didn't know of their execution he never inquired of their whereabouts. For their loyalty they were treated like pawns in a game of chess.

In order to get rid of Hamlet in a different manner he organised a duel between Hamlet and Laertes. Laertes was the son of Polonius who had been killed by Hamlet and Claudius arranged the duel so that it looked like Laertes was getting revenge for his father's death. Usually a duel was fought with a blade with a blunt tip but Claudius made sure that the blade of Laertes's sword was sharpened and had poison on it. If this didn't work he had a cup of poisoned wine ready for Hamlet to drink, the wine Gertrude drank. The fact that Claudius had everything so meticulously planned proves that he acted not out of insanity but pure calculated hate and evil.

Laertes, like Rosencrantz and Guildenstern, was another of Claudius's pawns and also died for his efforts. Polonius had been very loyal to Claudius, had welcomed his rule, and had spied on Hamlet for him, even using his daughter Ophelia as bait.

When Hamlet killed Polonius the only thing that Claudius cared about was not the death of a loyal subject but that he wouldn't be blamed for the murder.

Claudius deserved to be killed by Hamlet not just in revenge for King Hamlet's death but because he had ruined so many lives. He was a corrupt leader who did nothing good for his country and his corruption is shown in the quote from one of the guards: 'Something is rotten in the state of Denmark.'

I think he was justly punished for the murder of his brother. It's just a pity that his death hadn't been slower and more painful like the other deaths he caused.

P: 16/18
C: 14/18
L: 13/18
M: 6/6
Total: 49/60

Comments from the Department of Education and Science:
- Has good sense of the task set.
- Argues coherently.
- Illustration might be more sharply focused on the text.

COMMENTS/POINTS TO NOTE

The answer could be improved by more detailed reference to the actual text and by quoting to support the points made in each paragraph. Some of the syntax and language used is a little awkward in places.

This question and the comments that follow are taken from www.examinations.ie, the section entitled 'Chief Examiners' Reports 2005'.

Question

In your opinion, what is the appeal of the play, *Hamlet*, for a twenty-first-century audience? Support the points you make by reference to the text. (2005)

ANSWER

In my opinion, there are many different ways in which Hamlet appeals to a twenty-first-century audience. Through the setting, plot and language may be centuries old, the themes of the piece are universal, and the character of Hamlet still resonates today.

Though the setting of a royal court some time previous to the 1600s and the plot involving ghosts and vengeance may seem archaic to someone unfamiliar with the text, the themes explored in the play are universal, and still have relevance in the modern world.

One of these themes is that of duty to family. Hamlet's quest is driven by his father's story—of his own murder—and his request—to avenge his death. As he bids Hamlet 'Remember me', he charges Hamlet with the task of 'fixing' the situation—which Hamlet is originally reluctant to do: 'O cursed spite/That ever I was born to set it right!' Whilst the specifics of the situation are unlikely to occur again, almost everybody has at some point been placed in a situation where they felt duty bound to assist a family member, whether at their own asking, as with the Ghost, or through another's implication, as when Claudius asks Laertes, 'Did you love your father?'

The theme of family is also still highly relevant in modern times, in fact, with divorce rates steeply on the rise, never has the idea of 'family' been more relevant. Initially, Hamlet's dislike for Claudius is unrelated to his father's murder (though the line 'O my prophetic soul!' implies he had considered it), but he is still vehement in his hatred of the new king—particularly in comparison to his father: 'Hyperion to a satyr'. Purely from Hamlet's words, we are presented with a thoroughly negative view of the new king, though at this point, little evidence from the play supports this point of view. All Claudius's attempts to befriend Hamlet, or act in a fatherly manner are met with hostility and coldness. The ideas explored in this theme are still as relevant as ever.

And last, the theme of revenge still has as much relevance and appeal as ever. Whilst we may not seek revenge in the same manner as in Elizabethan times, the idea of revenge is still relevant. The lengths to which the three avengers in the play, Hamlet, Laertes and to a lesser extent Fortinbras are willing to go to gain revenge still holds a large appeal for a modern audience. The deception and deceitfulness practised by the characters in these endeavours—particularly those of Claudius and Laertes in their attempts to poison Hamlet—are still as relevant as always—one need only watch any soap opera on television to see these themes and actions still being used to great effect for the entertainment of the masses.

The second reason I believe the play 'Hamlet' still has appeal in the twenty-first century is because of the character of Hamlet himself. He is not a shining, perfect hero, but a character with deep flaws and a tendency towards unlikeable behaviour. Though he is described to us by Ophelia and Horatio, arguably the only innocent characters in the play, as being a 'just man' and in possession of a 'noble mind' and other good qualities—duty to his father and philosophical and educated mind, one often overshadowed by his neuroses, anger and cruelty. He is neurotic concerning his father's death and mother's remarriage, unable to speak reasonably on the subject, and damning all women on the basis of his mother's failings: 'Frailty, thy name is woman.' This neurosis also drives him to violence and anger, particularly in his conversation with Gertrude in her bed chamber. Many productions feature him assaulting Gertrude in this scene, holding her roughly and forcing her to look where he instructs. His anger also causes Polonius's death as he kills him without knowing who he was, and finally he says he shall 'lug the guts into the neighbour room', and the 'noble mind' referenced earlier has surely been 'o'er thrown'. Finally, his cruelty to Ophelia shows great callousness. He has made many 'offerings of love' to her, but, his mind coloured by his mother's sins, he cannot see her purity, only the 'frailty' he now believes is inherent in all women. Not only does he ignore her next advances, he denies ever loving her 'not I, I never gave you ought', and abuses her verbally, calling her a future 'breeder of sinners' and tells her to 'get thee to a nunnery.'

Though Hamlet has his strengths, his weaknesses make him more appealing as a character, and along with the universal themes within the play, this is what makes the play 'Hamlet' still appealing to a twenty-first-century audience.

P: 17/18
C: 14/18
L: 16/18
M: 5/6
Total: 52/60

Comments:

- Well-structured answer, good focus on the task.
- Effective use of illustration from the text.
- Points might be developed more fully on occasion.
- Some flaws in expression and mechanics.

COMMENTS/POINTS TO NOTE

This is quite a substantial answer to the question. The writer makes many relevant references to where and how this play is relevant to a twenty-first-century audience. The answer also takes a clear stance on the question and it outlines to the reader where the answer is going.

There are some confusing statements and some ambiguous expressions which prevent it from getting that higher mark.

QUESTIONS ON *HAMLET*

PAST LEAVING CERTIFICATE QUESTIONS

1. 'In Hamlet, all the major characters, either by chance or force of circumstances, play roles against which they inwardly revolt.' In the case of two of the major characters consider the dramatic effects of this internal conflict. Make reference to or quotation from the play. (1976)
2. 'The Hamlet who returns to Denmark in Act V can be at all points distinguished from his earlier passionate, indecisive and unpredictable self. He is a new man.' Discuss, using quotation and reference from the play. (1976)
3. 'In the play, *Hamlet*, Shakespeare's portrayal of women is not very flattering.' Discuss with reference to Gertrude and Ophelia. Make reference to or quotation from the play. (1980)
4. 'Hamlet's killing of Polonius in Act III scene iv is an important turning point in the action of the play.' Discuss, using quotation and reference from the play. (1980)
5. 'Loyalty and betrayal are significant themes in Shakespeare's *Hamlet*.' Discuss, using quotation and reference from the play. (1984)
6. Discuss the importance of the role of Fortinbras in the play. Make reference to or quotation from the play. (1984)
7. 'The fascination of the character, Hamlet, lies in the fact that he ranges from subtle reflections on morality and life, to violent and cynical action and back again.' Discuss, using quotation and reference from the play. (1988)
8. 'The interaction of plot and subplot gives pointed emphasis to the theme of filial duty in Hamlet.' Discuss, using quotation and reference from the play. (1988)
9. Discuss the importance of the character Horatio in the play *Hamlet*. Make reference to or quotation from the play. (1992)
10. 'Horror and disgust at his mother's behaviour, and a spreading and deepening of that horror and disgust to include all life, dominate the soul of Hamlet.' Discuss this view of Hamlet's character. Make reference to or quotation from the play. (1992)
11. 'There are many comic moments in Shakespeare's *Hamlet*.' Discuss this statement, supporting your points by reference to the text. (2000)

SOME GENERAL QUESTIONS

1. 'It is impossible to see anything heroic in Hamlet.' Do you think this is a fair

assessment of Hamlet's character? Support your answer by reference to or quotation from the play.

2. Discuss the dramatic purpose and role of the Ghost in *Hamlet*. Support your points by quotation or reference to the play.

3. Discuss the importance of Gertrude in the play. Support your answer by quotation or reference to the play.

4. Discuss the theme of revenge in Shakespeare's *Hamlet*. Support your answer by reference to the play.

5. 'Hamlet is a gloomy play, which leaves us with a very pessimistic view of life.' Do you agree with this statement? Support your answer by quotation or reference to the play.

6. Discuss the importance of Ophelia and Laertes in the play. Support your answer by reference or quotation from the play.

7. 'The Closet Scene marks a turning point in Hamlet's mindset.' Discuss this statement.

8. 'The female characters in the play are victims of the crimes and follies of the men.' Do you agree with this view? Support your answer by reference to the play.

9. What relevance has the play to a modern audience? Make reference to or quotation from the play.

10. Discuss the function of the soliloquy in the play.

11. 'The Play Scene is the central point of *Hamlet*. It is the climax and the crisis of the whole drama.' Discuss this view.

12. 'I am but mad north-north-west. When the wind is southerly I know a hawk from a handsaw.' How mad, in your opinion, is Hamlet? Support your answer by reference to the play.

13. Would you agree that the world of Elsinore is a depressingly masculine and brutal one, in which the women play subservient and ineffective roles?

14. 'Every society produces a different staging of *Hamlet* to reflect its own concerns.' What aspects of this play do you think should be emphasised in a contemporary production?

15. *Hamlet* is a play full of questions. What, in your opinion, are its most important questions, and how do you think the play answers any or all of them?

16. Would you agree that the themes are powerfully revealed in the rich imagery of the play? Support your points by quotation or reference to the play.

17. Choose two minor characters in the play and discuss what they contribute to the action and what they represent in the play.

18. Comment on the emphasis on death in *Hamlet*.

19. Identify your favourite scene in the play and outline the reasons why you like it so much.

DEPARTMENT OF EDUCATION GUIDELINES ON ANSWERING LEAVING CERT QUESTIONS

MARKING SCHEME

Mark ex 60 by reference to the criteria for assessment using the following breakdown of marks:

Purpose (P): 18 marks.

Coherence (C): 18 marks.

Language (L): 18 marks.

Mechanics (M): 6 marks.

2001

> 1. 'The struggle between Hamlet and Claudius is a fascinating one.' Discuss this statement, supporting your answer by reference to the play *Hamlet*.

Allow for an implicit treatment of 'fascinating' and a liberal interpretation of its meaning. Expect a clear focus on the **nature** of the conflict between the characters, rather than a mere re-telling of the course of the conflict.

    Code H/C for the 'struggle between Hamlet and Claudius'.

Possible Points

- The conflict is a fascinating one because . . .
- It is sustained throughout the play.
- It is a struggle between 'mighty opposites'—the stakes are so high.
- It is a moral struggle as well as a physical one.
- It is a very exciting contest—a battle of wits.
- It occasionally has its funny side—the weapon of the 'antic disposition'.
- It reveals a family at war.
- It takes the form of a criminal investigation.

> 2. Choose the scene from Shakespeare's *Hamlet* that in your view was the most dramatic. Discuss your choice, supporting your answer by reference to the play. (Textual support may include reference to a particular performance of the play you have seen.)

Allow a liberal interpretation of 'dramatic', to include 'exciting' or 'interesting' or 'entertaining', etc.

Expect a clear focus on the reason/s why the candidate found the chosen scene to be dramatic.

Code D for dramatic.

Possible Points
- The scene is full of conflict.
- There is tension and suspense aplenty.
- The scene contains interesting action and incident.
- There are interesting characters/relationships present.
- The scene involves sudden changes of pace or mood.
- The presence of great poetry.
- The scene dramatises an important theme.
- There was dramatic use of props, costume, lighting, music, special effects, etc.

2002

> 1. 'The appeal of Shakespeare's *Hamlet* lies primarily in the complex nature of the play's central character, Hamlet.' To what extent would you agree with the above statement? Support your points by reference to the play.

The thoroughness of the engagement with the complex nature of Hamlet's character will constitute an implicit treatment of 'the appeal' of the play.

Code CH for the 'complex nature' of Hamlet.

Candidates may disagree with the statement, but in doing so they must maintain a focus on the play's central character.

Possible Points
- His character is multi-faceted.
- He plays many roles in the play—lover, poet, prince, avenger, philosopher.

- His emotional complexity.
- He is elusive, enigmatic.
- His behaviour is frequently at odds with his words/thoughts.
- His complexity is bewildering, confusing, inconsistent.
- His contradictions are evidence of Shakespeare's artistic failure.

---

2. What is your view of the importance of either Gertrude or Ophelia in Shakespeare's *Hamlet*? Support the points you make by reference to the text.

Expect the candidates' responses to focus on the role/function/importance of the chosen character rather than simply offer descriptions/character sketches.

In the unlikely event that a candidate writes about **both** Gertrude and Ophelia, treat the answer as two separate attempts and assess them accordingly.

Code GI for the importance of Gertrude and OI for the importance of Ophelia.

Possible Points
Gertrude:
- As a key adjunct to Claudius, she is centrally important to the plot.
- She is significantly linked with Hamlet.
- Her 'falling off' shapes Hamlet's attitude to life and to women.
- She embodies key themes in the play.
- She is a significant presence on the stage.
- She gives rise to many questions in the minds of the audience.

Ophelia:
- Although she plays a comparatively small part, she has a major influence on the emotional life of the central character.
- Her exploitation by others is symptomatic of the world of the play.
- Her innocence and purity heighten our sense of the corruption about her.
- She draws forth our pity and sympathy.
- Her real madness counterpoints Hamlet's feigned madness.

2005

> 1. In your opinion, what is the appeal of the play *Hamlet* for a twenty-first-century audience? Support the points you make by reference to the text.

Candidates may argue that Hamlet does/does not appeal to, or draws mixed reactions from, the modern audience or reader.

Expect discussion to focus on at least one aspect of the play in support of the argument being made. A clear engagement with the appeal of the play will constitute implicit treatment of the response of a 'twenty-first-century audience'.

Code A for 'appeal' and A for 'does not appeal'.

Possible Points

The play is appealing because of:
- the relevance of its themes—it is a timeless narrative
- the variety of its characters and action
- the powerful central figure of Hamlet
- its language, imagery
- its dramatic intensity.

The play does not appeal because of:
- its complex plot, confusingly detailed
- its improbable events
- the outmoded world, an outdated revenge story.

> 2. 'We admire Hamlet as much for his weaknesses as for his strengths.'
> Write a response to this view of the character of Hamlet, supporting your points by reference to the text.

Expect candidates to maintain a focus on the strength(s) and weakness(es) of Hamlet's character and on their admiration or otherwise of those strengths and weaknesses.

In outlining their responses to the question candidates may well employ focused narrative to illustrate the points they make.

Code AW for 'admire weakness' and AS for 'admire strength'. Candidates may disagree in whole or in part with the thesis of the question, in which case code AW—for 'do not admire weakness' and AS—for 'do not admire strength/s'.

Where candidates address our admiration of Hamlet's weaknesses and/or strengths in an indirect or implicit way, code W for 'weakness' and S for 'strength.'

Interpret 'admire' liberally to mean 'to enjoy,' 'to be fascinated by,' 'to be interested in,' 'to find remarkable or important', and so on.

Possible Points

We enjoy:
- his intelligence, his wit, his words
- his insight into life and death.

We admire:
- his loyalty to his father and to his friends
- his bravery in taking on the state
- his recklessness
- the strategist.

We are fascinated by:
- his heroic failure
- his response to his traumatic experiences
- the profundity of his thinking
- his complex response to a difficult task
- the deviousness of his mind even though his actions cause others to suffer.

We find interesting:
- his ability to improvise as in the play within a play
- his rashness which leads him into further trouble
- his procrastination because we see ourselves reflected in it.

But we disapprove of:
- his cruelty to others
- his aimlessness
- his tendency to find refuge in words
- his self-loathing, his despair
- his treatment of women
- his impulsiveness
- his fondness for melodrama.